Coaching
CONVERSATIONS

To Arthur—my Muse
To Alyssa, Brittney, Riley, Orianna,
Jackie, and Ellie—our hope for the future

Coaching
CONVERSATIONS

Transforming
Your
School

One
Conversation
at a Time

Linda Gross Cheliotes
Marceta Fleming Reilly

Foreword by
Dennis Sparks

CORWIN
A SAGE Company

For information:

Corwin
A SAGE Company
2455 Teller Road
Thousand Oaks,
    California 91320
(800) 233-9936
Fax: (800) 417-2466
www.corwin.com

SAGE India Pvt. Ltd.
B 1/I 1 Mohan Cooperative
    Industrial Area
Mathura Road,
New Delhi 110 044
India

SAGE Ltd.
1 Oliver's Yard
55 City Road
London EC1Y 1SP
United Kingdom

SAGE Asia-Pacific Pte. Ltd.
33 Pekin Street #02-01
Far East Square
Singapore 048763

Printed in the United States of America

Library of Congress Cataloging-in-Publication Data

Coaching conversations : transforming your school one conversation at a time / authors, Linda Gross Cheliotes, Marceta Fleming Reilly; foreword by Dennis Sparks.
    p. cm.
Includes bibliographical references and index.
ISBN 978-1-4129-8183-5 (pbk.)
    1. School improvement programs. 2. Communication in education.
3. Communication in management. I. Cheliotes, Linda Gross. II. Reilly, Marceta Fleming. III. Title.

LB2822.8.C63 2010
371.2'07—dc22   2010001678

This book is printed on acid-free paper.

10   11   12   13   14   10   9   8   7   6   5   4   3   2   1

Acquisitions Editor:	Arnis Burvikovs
Associate Editor:	Joanna Coelho
Production Editor:	Amy Schroller
Copy Editor:	Tomara Kafka
Typesetter:	C&M Digitals (P) Ltd.
Proofreader:	Charlotte J. Waisner
Indexer:	Sylvia Coates
Cover Designer:	Karine Hovsepian

Contents

Foreword

The "coach-like" conversations recommended by Linda Gross Cheliotes and Marceta Fleming Reilly in *Coaching Conversations: Transforming Your School One Conversation at a Time* are an incredibly powerful and often underestimated means of promoting improvements in teaching, learning, and relationships in schools. Gross Cheliotes' and Reilly's view represents a significant paradigm shift regarding the role of the leader in promoting professional learning and cultural change. Conversations like the ones you will learn about in this book can alter beliefs, deepen understanding, energize and guide the school community, and strengthen practice.

When I first learned about "life coaching" more than a decade ago, I realized that the attributes displayed by life coaches would be an important and useful addition to the skill set of school leaders as they navigated the web of relationships that comprise the core of their work. It simply made good sense, I concluded, to teach the most important of those skills to school leaders, a process that is the subject matter of this useful and practical book. Such teaching when done well and followed by persistent practice creates new habits that leaders can apply in chance hallway conversations with teachers, in professional meetings, and in various kinds of interactions with students and parents.

There is an important caveat, however, to the increased use of conversations as a leadership tool: Not all conversations are created equal in their ability to promote professional learning and to stimulate individual and group change. The kinds of conversations described in *Coaching Conversations* share several characteristics. First, they are intentional. They have as their goal deeper understanding, stronger relationships, and a commitment to action that is sustained over time. Second, skillful conversations are grounded in deep and mindful listening that honors the speaker's perspective and demonstrates a willingness to be influenced by what others have to say. And third, skillful conversations are candid, leading to higher levels of trust and interpersonal accountability.

Conversely, such conversations can be defined by what they are not. They are not disguised "command and control" methods of influence by which administrators issue directives and use fear and force to mandate compliance to those directives. Skillful conversations are not "serial speech making" in which one person after another delivers well-rehearsed monologues to a disengaged audience. Nor are they manipulative. Because they are intentional and candid, skillful conversations are straightforward with no hidden agendas.

My views about conversation-based learning and mutual influence are based on several assumptions. I encourage readers to examine their own beliefs in these areas as a first step in fully engaging with the ideas and practices recommended by the authors.

- *Clear intentions are a precursor to improvement.* It's hard to make things better if you don't know what you want to accomplish.
- *Leaders' clarity is a precursor to continuous improvement in teaching and learning.* Good conversations help leaders develop clarity regarding intentions, values, ideas, and practices while promoting clarity throughout the school community.
- *Clarity cannot be "delivered" to others.* Clarity is achieved by grappling with the topic at hand until "brains are changed" and learning has occurred. Good conversations promote learning through a sustained focus and an ever-deepening consideration of important subjects.

- *Just-in-time learning is particularly potent because it is connected to real-life challenges and is motivated by a "need to know."* Good conversations by their very nature focus on the here-and-now reality of participants and generate clarity about and energy for future actions.
- *Leaders' hopefulness and positive attitudes are contagious.* Whether they intend it or not, leaders infect others with their emotions and attitudes. Good conversations create *positivity*—through conversation members of the school community develop a sense of possibility about the future and are energized to maintain the momentum of the change process.

Coaching Conversations: Transforming Your School One Conversation at a Time is worthy of careful study. I encourage you to examine its ideas and consider how its many examples may apply to your unique responsibilities. Most of all, I urge you to diligently practice the skills Gross Cheliotes and Reilly describe until they become new habits of mind and behavior. The result will almost certainly be significant changes in yourself and improvements in the quality of your day-to-day interactions with others and in your school's culture. Together those changes form the bedrock of significant and permanent improvements in teaching and learning in your school.

—*Dennis Sparks*

Dennis Sparks is president of Thinking Partners in Ann Arbor, Michigan. For 23 years he served as executive director of the National Staff Development Council. He can be reached at dennis.sparks@comcast.net.

Preface

*C*oaching Conversations: Transforming Your School One Conversation at a Time* provides a simple guidebook for school leaders that will introduce you to effective coaching conversation skills, which are critical for making systemic change. These skills will significantly increase your ability to engage and motivate the members of your school communities as you work collaboratively toward total school transformation. By investing a minimal amount of time to learn and practice the valuable conversational skills outlined in this book, you will experience a significant return on your investment.

Michael Fullan's research (2006) demonstrates the importance of motivating people to change and grow through relationships based on treating others with dignity and respect. We advocate that coach-like conversations focus on building relationships through committed listening, asking powerful questions that result in deeper thinking, and utilizing reflective feedback that holds each person to high standards while at the same time preserves their personal dignity.

Charles Payne (2008) establishes the case for relational trust as the most important factor in moving the lowest tier schools to higher levels of achievement. Through ongoing, respectful coaching conversations, space is provided for personal and professional growth and change within a framework of relational trust.

The content we share in this book is based on the training materials we use in our Coaching For Results, Inc., workshops. Many people in CFR have contributed to the ideas, examples, figures, and text of its content. The examples and running dialogues we use throughout the book come from our work with school leaders. The names of the people and some of the details of the situations have been changed to protect their confidentiality.

Coaching Conversations: Transforming Your School One Conversation at a Time was written for school leaders at all organizational levels. School leaders include principals and their assistants, directors, superintendents, professional development personnel, and also teachers in leadership roles, such as instructional coaches, content specialists, and lead teachers. Anyone within the school community whose role focuses on collaboration with others will be able to learn and practice the skills described in this book to transform their schools, their departments, their grade levels, or their districts.

In the first chapter you will learn what distinguishes a coaching conversation from other interactions and how coaching conversations may transform your school community.

Chapter 2 distinguishes in greater detail how coaching conversations differ from supervisory and mentoring conversations. In addition, you will learn the importance of using coach-like conversational practices even when your goal for a particular conversation may be focused on serious supervisory concerns.

The goal of Chapter 3 is learning and developing committed listening skills, which are foundational to holding genuine coaching conversations and building relational trust. Until you truly understand by listening to both the words and essence of what another person is saying meaningful dialogue and change is unlikely to occur.

In Chapter 4 you will learn the importance of speaking powerfully, which includes forming a specific intention for speaking, choosing words that align with your inner thoughts, and entering the conversation with positive intentions about the other person. You will also learn to use open-ended questions that provoke deep thinking by other people, which helps them generate possibilities that lead to actions.

Chapter 5 introduces the reader to a very specific form of speaking called reflective feedback. This useful framework offers several options for delivering meaningful feedback. It can also be used to Coach-on-the-Fly as well as to structure a conversation about a difficult topic.

Finally, in Chapter 6 you will read two authentic case studies that demonstrate the transformative power of coaching conversations. The first example describes a single coaching conversation that shows how significant insight and the beginnings of change are possible, even within the short timeframe of a single conversation. The second case study allows the reader to witness the progression toward growth and change of a school leader who has been engaged in a series of conversations with her coach over a period of several months.

Transforming your school through coaching conversations requires dedicated practice of the skills outlined in this book. At the same time, utilizing these skills must be done authentically and honestly or people may feel manipulated or that the conversation is superficial. In other words, when coaching conversations are sincere, there is a high probability that trust will grow between the participants and that pathways for growth and change will develop.

We have written this book because we have seen amazing transformations occur in school leaders as they think deeply about what they want, get clear about their purposes, and practice the effective communication skills we promote in this book. We believe that when put into practice, coach-like conversations have the power to transform school cultures and impact the quality of the school experience for all children.

Acknowledgments

Many people influenced and supported the writing of *Coaching Conversations: Transforming Your School One Conversation at a Time*. We are grateful to our coaching colleagues in Coaching For Results, Inc., for their inspiration, support, and wisdom. We are especially thankful to Kathy Kee, Karen Anderson, Frances Shuster, Diana Williams, and Edna Harris for much of the development of the training materials and seminars on which this book is based. Their insights and knowledge have been invaluable.

In addition, we want to acknowledge Dave Ellis for his creative work and his generosity through the Brande Foundation, which has supported the transformation of countless people through the training and work of numerous life coaches, including many founding members of Coaching For Results, Inc.

Dennis Sparks, Stephanie Hirsh, and Joellen Killion, from the National Staff Development Council, first envisioned bringing coaching to school leaders. Their encouragement and support continues to fuel our work.

We acknowledge and thank our coaching clients who have not only provided examples for this book but also contributed to our personal growth and knowledge by teaching us effective ways to support people to lead major change initiatives within their schools and their lives.

To our families who have supported and encouraged our efforts, we offer our sincere appreciation and love for their understanding and patience.

Additionally, Corwin gratefully acknowledges the following peer reviewers for their editorial insight and guidance:

Sean Beggin
Assistant Principal
Andover High School
Andover, MN

Patricia Bowman
Retired Administrator and
    Independent Educational
    Consultant
Inglewood, CA

Roberta Glaser
Assistant Superintendent
    (Retired)
St. Johns Public Schools
St. Paul, MI

Harriet Gould
Adjunct Professor in
    Educational
    Administration
Concordia University
Fallbrook Campus
Lincoln, NE

Lynn Macan
Superintendent
Cobleskill-Richmondville
    Central School
Cobleskill, NY

Rob Slauson
Principal
Lincoln Southwest
    High School
Lincoln, NE

Dana Salles Trevethan
Principal
Turlock High School
Turlock, CA

Bonnie Tryon
President of SAANYS and
    Principal Instructional
    Planning and Support
Cobleskill-Richmondville
    Central Schools
Cobleskill, NY

Paul Young
Executive Director
West After School
    Center, Inc.
Lancaster, OH

About the Authors

Linda Gross Cheliotes, EdD, has more than 38 years of successful educational experience, including 14 years as a school administrator. As principal, she transformed her underperforming school to a National Blue Ribbon School of Excellence. Dr. Gross Cheliotes was named a National Distinguished Principal in 2002 and holds a doctorate in Organizational Leadership.

For the past two years, Dr. Gross Cheliotes has been a coach and trainer with Coaching For Results, Inc., a national consortium of school leadership coaches. She is a founding member and coach for the National Association of Elementary School Principals (NAESP) principal mentor certification program. Dr. Gross Cheliotes currently works with the New York City Council of School Supervisors and Administrators' Executive Leadership Institute, providing professional development for assistant principals who aspire to become principals. She has presented numerous professional development programs at the national, state, and local levels.

Dr. Gross Cheliotes is a member of the International Coach Federation and NAESP and an Associate Certified Coach (ACC).

Marceta Fleming Reilly, PhD, has 42 years of experience in education, moving from teacher to principal to school superintendent in Kansas. Her vision and passion were to create schools that were welcoming to students and families, and centers of learning and success for the entire community.

Dr. Reilly is now a leadership coach and has the Professional Certified Coach (PCC) credential from the International Coach Federation. She is a founding member of Coaching For Results, Inc., and dedicated to partnering with school leaders who are doing transformational work. She uses coaching conversations to help her clients gain insight and confidence, and she helps build their capacity to be extraordinary leaders, based on their individual, innate strengths.

Dr. Reilly regularly conducts workshops about coaching conversations. She is a frequent speaker at state and national conferences and has been invited to present these ideas to audiences in China (2007) and India (2009).

Coaching Conversations

The Link to Change

While no conversation is guaranteed to change the trajectory of a career, a company, a relationship or a life— any single conversation can.

—Susan Scott, *Fierce Conversations*

School leaders face many challenges and wear a variety of hats during the course of one school day. In addition to the day-to-day management of a large organization, they handle numerous tasks that never appear on their daily schedules. As they walk through their schools, leaders may notice a leak in a ceiling pipe, informally discuss instructional practices with teachers and other staff, help a pair of students settle a dispute, and then receive a message to return to the office immediately for an important telephone call from the superintendent or a parent.

The school community expects their leaders to be visionary, have deep knowledge about effective instruction and curriculum, create a peaceful and productive learning environment, interact with community businesses and agencies, manage limited resources carefully, and be readily available at a moment's notice to handle emergencies, respond to questions, attend meetings, and develop plans.

In this chapter you will learn

- What coaching conversations entail
- How coaching conversations support findings from brain research
- Why some conversations are difficult
- How to move toward coaching conversations

One thing is certain about the role of a school leader—it is people intensive! Dynamic school leaders not only have the knowledge and skills to manage their schools and understand the components of effective instruction, they are also outstanding communicators. They develop a strong vision and make decisions that impact their school community. However, a vision is a lifeless document unless the school leader clearly articulates and gets buy-in for this vision from staff, parents, students, and community members. A principal may delineate a multistep action plan for school improvement, but sustained growth and change are not likely to occur unless all constituencies of the school accept the plan as their own and feel supported as they implement new initiatives.

Typically school leaders have several formal opportunities during the year for professional development leading to school transformation. There may be specific professional development days on the school's calendar and some staff members may participate in workshops provided elsewhere. In addition, many school leaders utilize full staff meetings and grade or department meetings as professional growth opportunities.

More important, during the course of a single day, school leaders have dozens of opportunities to effect change through short conversations with staff, students, parents, colleagues, supervisors, and community members. In *Coaching Conversations: Transforming Your School One Conversation at a Time,* our premise is that there are very specific coach-like skills that lead to organizational transformation—one person at a time.

What Is a Coaching Conversation?

Coaching conversations differ from typical, spur-of-the-moment conversations. First, they are highly intentional rather than just friendly or

> Coaching conversations are focused on the other person.

informal interactions. In addition, coaching conversations are focused on the other person—her strengths and her challenges, and the attributes she brings to the conversations. A third characteristic of coaching conversations is that their purpose is to stimulate growth and change. In other words, coaching conversations lead to action.

Of course, school leaders already employ a variety of conversational techniques to effect change. For example, they hold supervisory conferences with the goal of improving instruction. However, how often do these one-on-one interactions result in true change and growth at the organizational level? An individual staff member may change his surface behavior as required by his administrator, yet deep and lasting change is unlikely because the teacher's relationship with his administrator may now have taken a negative direction, evoking emotions of defensiveness, anxiety, mistrust, inadequacy, and possibly fear.

School leaders also engage in mentoring conversations. These interactions usually occur when someone is new to the organization or lacks experience in implementing new skills. As mentor, the school leader takes on the role of a knowledgeable veteran who shares her skills with others. Realistically, even when the school leader is highly knowledgeable and experienced, she is unable to fully support a colleague or staff member because no mentor has the exact same background, temperament, situation, or life experience of those she mentors.

Old Thinking Versus New Thinking

So why are conversations that lead to change and transformation so difficult to manage? First, recent brain research, including work by David Rock (2006), demonstrates that motivating ourselves or others to change requires changing our long-established brain patterns. Even when we recognize that specific changes are necessary, we revert to our old patterns of thinking and acting because we already have well-established channels for old thinking. We resist change neurologically!

New patterns of thinking that lead to changed behavior require deep reflection and intentional, ongoing practice in order to create and develop new neural pathways within the brain.

> Coaching conversations foster the deep reflection necessary to establish new thinking patterns.

Coaching conversations foster the deep reflection necessary to establish new thinking patterns. Moreover, when a school leader engages in coaching conversations with members of her school community, she provides the ongoing support for staff and others to practice new thinking skills and behaviors. This leads to real change, not just at the surface level, but also at the neurological level. Simply put, coaching conversations foster the development of new neural pathways in the brain, which then make changed behavior possible and long lasting.

Holding Difficult Conversations

A major reason why many conversations are so difficult is that each party in the interaction has a personal agenda. For example, in a typical supervisory conversation the school leader points out some aspect of a teacher's instructional or interpersonal practices that must be changed. The leader's agenda requires that the teacher change his behavior so that the teacher will become more effective. On the other hand, the teacher's agenda in this conversation frequently is to defend or justify his actions. He may acquiesce to the school leader's requirements, but his compliance is at the surface level and his resulting behavioral changes may be short lived, lasting only as long as the school leader continues to exert pressure on the staff member.

Sometimes our conversations are unproductive because neither party has enough information about the other person to understand the other's viewpoint. We fail to listen to each other's words, body language, and other unstated cues. Instead, we often prepare a response in our heads, let our thoughts wander to our own stories or judgments, or focus on a solution—even when we have not been asked to provide one! Poor listening skills may be the cause of a failed conversation.

Conversations become difficult, too, when we speak without choosing our words carefully. We put the other person in a defensive posture by asking questions for which the response is only *yes* or *no* and give specific advice or direction. How often have you walked away from a conversation that you thought would end positively, only to find yourself or the other person left feeling angry, frustrated, or disappointed? How we speak is critical in holding productive conversations.

Moving Toward Coaching Conversations

Coaching Conversations: Transforming Your School One Conversation at a Time provides school leaders with practical, hands-on skills for holding conversations that result in reflective thinking and real change at a

> Long-term change through coaching conversation requires ongoing, thoughtful, and intentional practice.

deep, substantive level. The skills and concepts presented in this book are straightforward on a cognitive level. Long-term change through coaching conversations, however, requires ongoing, thoughtful, and intentional practice until new neural pathways for thinking and behaving have been established. At that point, coaching conversations will become a way of being within you and your school community.

We have organized *Coaching Conversations: Transforming Your School One Conversation at a Time* with a progression of skills that help the reader understand what a coaching conversation is and how this type of interpersonal activity may lead to deep and lasting change within a school community. We suggest that readers follow the chapters in order, taking notes and reflecting about what resonates personally. For example, a school leader reading this book may recognize himself in one or more of the unproductive patterns of listening described in Chapter 3. He may also notice that when he is silent and allows others to think through their ideas, they tend to develop very creative plans. By reflecting as he reads, this leader now has some ideas of places to start learning how to conduct coaching conversations with members of his school community.

Next, we suggest that you pick one skill that you are willing to practice in either your professional or personal life. For example, you may wish to practice valuing silence as others speak with you. Select one person with whom you interact on a regular basis and intentionally focus your attention on that individual as she speaks. Instead of interrupting her discourse with a similar story of your own, listen deeply and fully to what she says. Notice her nonverbal cues and also be mindful of your own unproductive listening skills, such as judgmental or solution thinking. Allow natural pauses in the conversation rather than quickly responding when the other person completes a thought. In the few seconds of silence you provide, does she then share more thoughts perhaps at a deeper level?

After a few coach-like interactions, then you will be ready to set personal action goals related to a specific skill or a specific situation. For example, you may decide to focus on asking open-ended questions (a specific skill) when speaking with your own children. Instead of asking, "Did you clean your room?" you might say, "What are your plans for cleaning your room before dinnertime?" You may decide to tie a skill to a very specific situation, such as asking open-ended questions during postobservation conferences with teachers.

In this case, you would prepare several open-ended questions before the conferences. Examples might include:

- As you think about past successful lessons, what could you do to incorporate similar instructional techniques in future lessons so that your class will engage actively in their own learning?
- What resources would you need to move your instructional practices to an even higher level of effectiveness?
- In reflecting about today's lesson, what would you do the same and what would you modify? Why?
- Describe how your lesson activities relate to your objective of having your students utilize higher order thinking skills?

After you have selected your personal action goals related to a specific skill or situation, we recommend that you practice these action goals for at least one to two weeks. Note your own progress and reactions along the way. You might enter your reflections in a personal journal or share your thoughts with a trusted colleague or friend. Also note any changes you notice in others as you practice your new skills. How have the conversations changed? In what ways are others reacting to you? What changes are occurring in your relationships with others?

Once you are comfortable using one skill, set action goals for an additional skill and then practice this skill too. Focused practice will eventually generalize and become a habitual way of holding conversations with others and require less conscious effort.

Summary

In this chapter we have discussed why it is hard to change and have laid out a suggested framework for learning the skills for coaching conversations. These steps will significantly impact

the effectiveness of your leadership. Start small and act intentionally. Sometimes telling a loved one or trusted friend about
your new conversational goals provides incentive to follow
through on learning or reinforce coaching conversational
skills. Celebrate your successes rather than focus on times you
may forget your goals.

Think about when you learned a new skill, for example,
how to drive a car. Those first few practice sessions were probably a bit scary and you had to focus very deliberately on
what to do with your feet, hands, eyes, and ears. After much
practice, your driving skills became smoother and more auto-
matic. Your brain developed the neural pathways to drive an
automobile safely and individual, specific driving skills
dropped to a lower level of consciousness within your brain.
Now, you probably notice the specific skills required to drive
a vehicle safely only when faced with an unusual situation,
such as an impending collision. Suddenly your mind quickly
reviews all of the component parts of driving: "How hard
should I hit the brakes?" "Which direction should I turn the
steering wheel?" "Is everyone safe?"

Just as your driving skills have become habituated
through extensive practice, you will discover that dedicated
practice of coaching conversational skills will become part of
your natural way of interacting with others. Your individual
coaching conversations will transform both your relationships
and your school community.

2

The New Leadership Model

Leaders must have conversations that interrogate reality, provoke learning, tackle tough challenges, and enrich relationships.

—Susan Scott, *Fierce Conversations*

Coaching conversations are an essential tool for the 21st-century leader. Coaching is a way of listening and speaking to colleagues that assumes a belief that others are whole and capable. Others don't need to be "fixed." Coaches operate with an underlying assumption that giving advice to others undermines the confidence and self-worth of others. Coaching language helps leaders communicate this deep trust and belief in others.

In this chapter you will

- Distinguish between old and new models of leadership
- Learn how the Leadership Practices Continuum describes typical leader behaviors
- Understand the difference between coaching and mentoring
- Discover the benefits of being coach-like in your leadership

Coaching conversations require that leaders think of themselves as partners and collaborators rather than experts and bosses. Yet most leaders have been tapped for their positions because they have been "idea" people—ones who have had lots of expertise in a certain area and could get things done. They were seen as advisors and good directors. But being an *advisor* and *director* are part of the old leadership model. See Figure 2.1 below.

Figure 2.1   Old Leadership Model

- Military model; chain of command
- Directing and telling
- Little focus on developing capacity in others
- Delegating and holding people accountable with little guidance; if given the job you are expected to know how to do it
- High task, low relationship, and a culture of compliance
- Silos and fiefdoms
- Competition for resources; if you have something it means there is less for me
- Desire to control the situation
- Sharing information mostly on a need-to-know basis
- Making decisions without getting input from others

Old Leadership Model

The old leadership model assumes leaders are experts and will tell others what to do. They have the ideas, information, knowledge, and lead by directing the operations. They keep control of the situation and delegate only to people whom they assume have the skills and knowledge to get the job done. If the person to whom a task was delegated does not perform up to expectations, he or she is blamed for the failure— not the leader.

The upside of this model is that things get done efficiently, following the thinking of the leader. In addition, the old leadership model is predictable and works adequately within bureaucratic organizations. The downside is that it breeds competition—if you have resources then there is less for me to have. If your idea is recognized, my work is somehow diminished. Silos are created within the organization because individuals are trying to outshine others and protect their territory from being usurped by colleagues.

This model of leadership may be adequate for bureaucratic work cultures. It becomes less effective in school cultures that want to support collaborative teams, creative and critical thinking skills, and high relationships to connect with students. Schools require a new model of leadership. See Figure 2.2 below.

New Leadership Model

In the new leadership model, the leader does not know all the answers. The leader asks questions, listens to the content

Figure 2.2   New Leadership Model

- Asking, listening, then directing (in that order)
- Focus on personal growth
- Delegating, coaching, and modeling accountability
- High task, high relationship, and a culture of passionate engagement
- Sharing resources, collaborating, and partnering across function areas
- Open and transparent
- Respectful of different points of view
- Original thinking; exposing one's view of reality about issues

and underlying themes in the answers, and then is able to integrate the group's thinking into a vision and direction to which people respond. This kind of leadership taps into the thinking and passions of others by seeking to develop the strengths and interests of others. It is not one person who determines success; it is the group that creates success. This engenders a culture of continuous improvement for all and *shared* pride in achievements.

The irony is that people are usually picked for leadership roles because they are energetic experts—they know what to do and are not afraid to tell it to others. But the higher leaders go within an organization, the farther they are from the level where change must occur, and the less they can depend upon their ideas alone to make things happen. Author Marceta Fleming Reilly learned this lesson the hard way in her own career.

Marceta's Story

> I spent 20 years of my career wanting to be, studying to be, practicing for and finally being a school superintendent. I thought that being a superintendent meant that I would have the power to create a school district that was focused on children and a center of learning for the entire community. To my great surprise, as superintendent I had less power than in preceding jobs. I now had not one, but seven bosses (members of the board of education) and I only evaluated people at the director level—not the school level. If I was going to create this school district of my dreams, I was going to have to operate through influence, not edict.

This realization started me on a journey into looking for new leadership models. I began to study and learn ways to share leadership and build capacity in others. My purpose was to become an *influencer* rather then a director. Figure 2.3 shows how this movement in leadership practices often occurs.

Leadership Practices Continuum

Figure 2.3 shows the Leadership Practices Continuum, which describes typical leader behaviors. On the left is the *supervising zone* in which the leader gives advice, tells people what to do, solves people's problems, or asks loaded questions such as, "Have you thought about . . . ?" The leader is directing by taking control of the situation and deciding the course of action or giving strong suggestions about best solutions. The leader is the expert and knows what to do.

Moving to the right is the *mentoring zone*. This is a "softer" form of directing. The thinking is that if I teach others what I know, they will handle situations as well as I do. At its best, it teaches necessary skills and insights to people who are new to their roles or positions. At its worst, it tries to "clone oneself" so that the other person will act the way the mentor wants.

The mentor-leader spends time teaching others and offering options. Mentors often use the tools of storytelling and advising. They tell stories about what worked when they had that problem or issue. They advise others about best actions to take in a given situation. The mentor takes on the role of a "wise one" who guides another person to know what to do, based on the mentor's own thinking and experiences. This is very appropriate for working with novices. We believe it is not the best way to work with experienced and highly motivated staff.

On the right is the *coaching zone*. Here the leader gives up the mantle of being *expert* or *wise one* and becomes an equal partner and collaborator with others involved in solving problems. The leader uses effective communication, such as listening for underlying themes or assumptions, asking questions, posing possibilities, and pushing thinking so that clear and creative ideas emerge. Decisions are therefore co-created by the group—not by any one individual—as they openly share information and thinking.

Figure 2.3   Leadership Practices Continuum

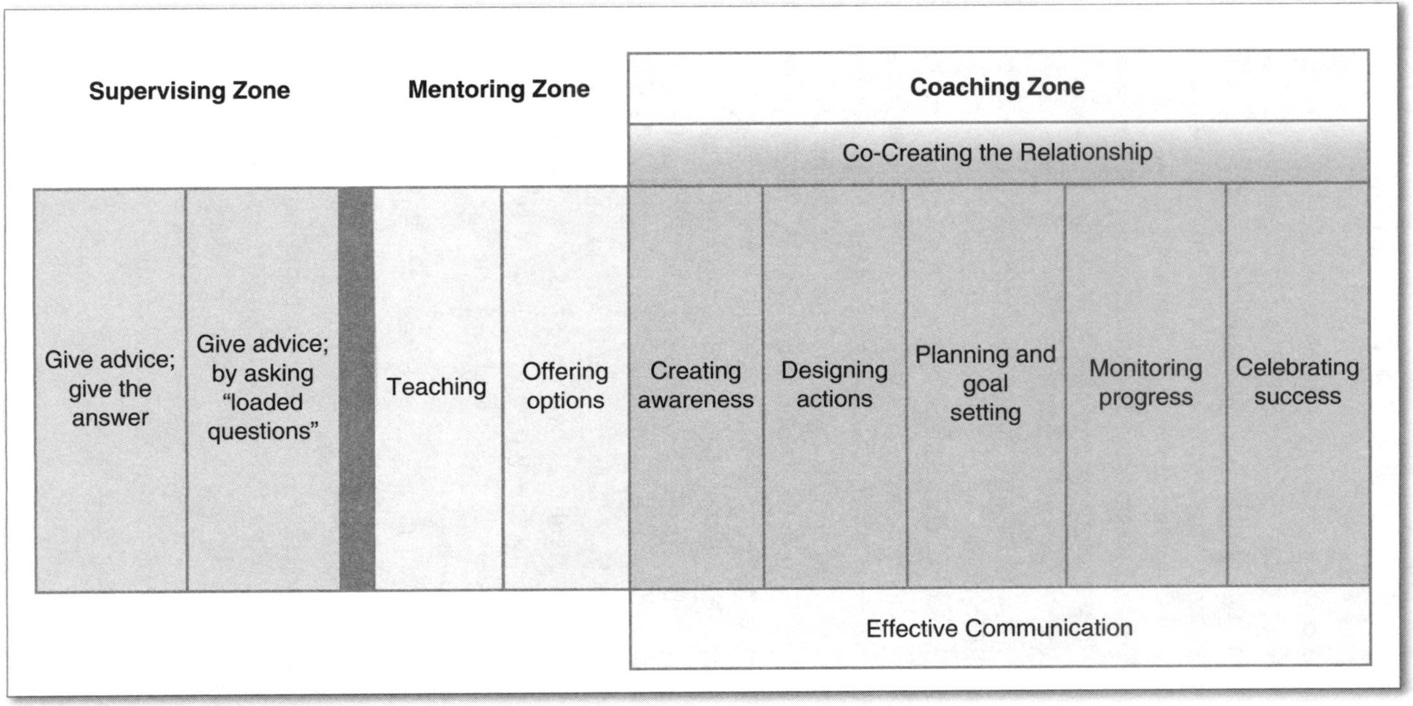

Supervising Zone		Mentoring Zone		Coaching Zone				
				Co-Creating the Relationship				
Give advice; give the answer	Give advice; by asking "loaded questions"	Teaching	Offering options	Creating awareness	Designing actions	Planning and goal setting	Monitoring progress	Celebrating success
				Effective Communication				

M. Reilly & D. Williams, 2008

How the Continuum Works in Practice

As you can see, we have strong beliefs about the power of coaching as an essential tool for school leaders in the 21st century. We believe that leaders should spend 85% of their time in the *coaching zone*, about 10% of their time in the *mentoring zone*, and only 5% of their time in the *supervising zone*. Working in the *coaching zone* should be the *first option* leaders use when they work with people. Coach-like leaders believe in others' abilities to grow and excel. They communicate through their coaching conversations that they see themselves as partners—not bosses. Leaders who are coach-like leave others feeling confident in themselves and appreciative of the support of their team. Coach-like leaders help others come up with *their own* best ideas. Notice in the following example, how the principal starts a difficult conversation from a coaching position.

> Coach-like leaders believe in others' abilities to grow and excel. They communicate through their coaching conversations that they see themselves as partners—not bosses.

Bonnie was principal of a large high school. She had three assistant principals who comprised the administrative team for her building. Bonnie was disturbed by the poor judgment of one of her new assistants, Walter, who had supervised an athletic event the previous Friday night. The basketball teams were fierce cross town rivals and after the game, a fight broke out in the parking lot. Students from both schools were involved in some serious punching, kicking, and name-calling. In the heat of breaking up the fight, Walter had yelled at the boys to "get your black asses off school property and go home."

Over the weekend Bonnie had received numerous calls from irate parents and board members who complained about Walter's racially charged comments. Rev. McCormick, pastor of the local community church, had requested a meeting with Bonnie to discuss the situation. The superintendent wanted an incident report on his desk by 9:00 AM Monday morning. Bonnie knew she needed to do something quickly to defuse this emotionally charged incident or else it would infect the entire learning atmosphere of the school for weeks to come.

Bonnie called Walter and asked him to meet her at her office on Saturday afternoon. When he arrived she asked him to explain what had happened the previous night. Walter was very upset and remorseful about how the events had escalated so quickly. He explained the standard procedures he had tried to use to stop the fighting at first. When that did not work, he lost his head and just "cussed them out."

Bonnie explained the consequences for making such an inappropriate comment and asked what he had thought about doing to make things right again. She noted that he had broken the community's trust, and he (actually, all the administrative team members) would have to take some action to earn back that trust. "If you were in the community's shoes, what would you want to see happen as a result of this incident?" she asked.

Walter was quiet for a while. Finally he spoke. "I would want a sincere apology from me for my bad behavior. I would want a local committee convened to review the school policies and procedures for handling student fights and give input about possible improvements. I would like assurances that there would be increased supervision and security at events involving large crowds and rival teams."

Over the next hour, Bonnie and Walter worked together to formulate a plan to do all the things Walter had suggested. They contacted the other two members of the administrative team and got their commitment to assist as well. By Monday afternoon Bonnie had called a press conference. The superintendent, Rev. McCormick, Bonnie, and the other administrative team members were all on the dais when Walter publicly apologized. The superintendent announced a community task force to review all policies and procedures related to student discipline. Bonnie assured the public that she would assign additional supervisory staff for local events drawing large numbers of students and she welcomed collaboration with local law enforcement to provide more security for the outside areas of the campus.

Bonnie could have called Walter in and reprimanded him severely for causing the explosive situation. She could have let Walter take all the blame and distanced herself from him. That would have been following the old model of leadership. Instead, Bonnie demonstrated the new model of leadership. She was coach-like as she listened to his story of the events, heard the remorse in his voice, and chose to work with him to rebuild and strengthen trust with community members.

When leaders are coach-like, they let go of always having the "right" answer. Instead, they support others in taking action toward their own goals. Walter's goals were to take some actions to heal the hurt he had caused within the community.

Rather than being judgmental, a coach-like leader helps others plan, reflect, problem solve, and make their own decisions. The leader's conversation time is spent on mediating resources, clarifying intentions, and identifying multiple options to assist others in self-directed learning and getting the optimal results they want.

Bonnie supported Walter's plan. She took responsibility for her part in not assigning more supervisors to the event. She made a commitment to continue to coach Walter as he worked with the community committee so that the broken trust could be repaired.

Being a Coach-Like Mentor

But what happens if people with whom a leader is working don't have enough background knowledge or experience to solve their problems or the solutions they are considering have some serious flaws? What if Walter did not know the importance of a public apology or the symbolic meaning of reviewing Board security policies? Then it is time for the leader to move back down the continuum to the *mentoring zone*. It would be time for Bonnie to suggest some key actions Walter could take to begin to help rebuild the public trust. She could say, "I'm thinking that a public apology will be necessary." Then wait to hear Walter's response. She could follow with, "What recommendations do you have to strengthen our security policies?" and "How could you assist a committee to help review these policies for the board of education so that these situations are less likely to happen in future?"

Yet even mentoring can be done using coach-like behaviors. Sharing the leader's knowledge and experience is very appropriate when it is within the context of helping the novices integrate the new learning into their own conceptual frameworks. The emphasis is on building capacity of the novices rather than on the leader being seen as an expert or guide. In this way the leader develops great trust and rapport with the novices without becoming a crutch, which could later damage their budding confidence.

Bernice is the mentor teacher in her school. When visiting one fifth-grade class, she noticed that the teacher, Jason, avoided involving his students in hands-on science experiments in the classroom, preferring to focus solely on the science text for lessons. Although Bernice could very easily have told Jason how to set up his classroom for hands-on experiments, her experience with coaching had taught her that it would be more valuable to elicit ideas and a plan from Jason than to tell him the steps directly.

Bernice made an appointment to visit Jason in his classroom while his students were in art class. Through a series of open-ended questions such as "I am wondering what would happen if you engaged your students in a short experiment about the water cycle?" Jason expressed concern about maintaining control of his students. When Bernice realized that Jason was worried that the children might misbehave if they were given a hands-on water activity to complete, she then asked him to describe what the ideal hands-on activity would look and sound like. Next Bernice asked Jason what steps he could take to ensure that his students stayed on task and worked with the materials in a responsible manner. Jason generated several ideas for organizing the class into small groups, assigning jobs for each group member during the experiment, and creating a form for each group to complete as they worked. By the end of their conversation, Jason felt confident about introducing the simple experiment he had discussed with Bernice.

Bernice could have mentored Jason by telling him her story about how successful she had been in using hands-on experiments with students. She could have told him how she organized the groups and kept them on task. While that would have informed Jason about what a great teacher

Bernice was, it would not necessarily have given him the confidence to do it just as she had.

Instead Bernice mentored Jason by drawing out his teaching preferences and strengths. She encouraged him to plan ways to gently ease into hands-on projects with students. She reinforced his confidence that he was capable of doing it and that she would be available to debrief about it afterward to make the lesson even better the next time.

On the other hand, when a staff member becomes passive-aggressive, insubordinate, or extremely difficult to work with, a leader can always be more forceful and directive by moving to the *supervisory zone*. Here the leader has to assert position power and clearly define requirements and non-negotiables in order to get simple compliance. Although these kinds of negative relationships can drain huge amounts of time and energy from a leader, they should only be necessary for 5% or less of a leader's staff.

The Case for Being Coach-Like

We believe that an overwhelming majority of people in our schools want to be effective and cooperative. Yet we do a disservice to this majority when a leader works with them in the supervising zone. Even if the leader is nice about it, the underlying assumptions of working in this zone are that there is one right answer, I am the expert, I know what is best, and my ideas and experiences count more than yours.

So should leaders give up directive leadership altogether, and not share their knowledge and experiences with others? The answer is yes and no.

- *Yes*, they should give up thinking of themselves as leaders who are expected to have all—and the best—answers and
- *No*, leaders *do* have solid knowledge and experiences that are very useful in planning and problem solving. So instead of *directing* they can channel their energies into

> Creating frames and posing "reframes" ramps up the thinking of the group while it models how to collaborate and professionally engage with colleagues.

posing parameters, norms, and criteria for the group to consider in their deliberations.

In other words, the knowledge and experience of leaders can create *frames* from which the best ideas emerge and decisions are made. Creating frames and posing "reframes" ramps up the thinking of the group while it models how to collaborate and professionally engage with colleagues.

The art teachers at Mount Hope Middle School had developed an outstanding program for students. It was a great source of pride for the students and the local community. More than half of the student body was involved in art classes, clubs, and activities. Students won many recognitions and awards as they displayed their work at businesses, community events, and competitions around the local area. A centerpiece for their program was periodic field trips that all the art students took to art shows, galleries, and museums. The problem was that the core subject teachers resented all the time these field trips were taking from their instruction. It meant that there were three to five days each year that they only had partial classes of students. It seemed like a waste of time to the core subject teachers—especially when the field trips did not connect with those important state tests.

Lloyd was assigned as the new principal at the school last year. Resentment and conflict among the staff around the art field trip issue had been brewing for several years and it did not take long for Lloyd to recognize this would be his first big test with the staff. Would he side with the core subject teachers or would he let the art teachers continue these field trips?

Lloyd had two goals for his first year: to establish a trusting relationship with his staff and to create a collaborative culture within his new school. So Lloyd decided to convene a committee of the art teachers and the teacher leaders for the core subjects. He gave this committee some ground rules for proposing a plan to resolve this issue.

Lloyd told the committee that the plan had to

1. *Reflect input from art teachers and the core subject teachers*

2. *Respect the traditions of the school (the art program was sacred to the community)*

3. *Respect instructional priorities as well as the interests of the students*

4. *Have collective consensus among all staff about the final decision*

Over the course of several weeks Lloyd worked with this leadership team to define clearer rules for all field trips within the school. The final rules seemed simple and as a result of working together, both the art teachers and the core subject teachers developed greater understanding and respect for each other.

Lloyd did not use his expertise to solve the problem. He set clear criteria by which the decision would be made and supported the team recommendation. He demonstrated his trust in his staff to resolve their own issues in productive ways. In using this process, he modeled collaboration and professionalism and he gained great appreciation from his staff about his "wisdom."

Summary

School leaders in the 21st century must help staff find creative and engaging ways to connect students with complex learning. The old model of leadership was sufficient for schools of the past, but the new demands of 21st-century leadership are best served by a new way of leading that models collaboration and transparency.

Leaders are often selected for leadership roles based on their individual success in the past. Yet when they become leaders, they need to learn new skills to build the capacity of others rather than trying to be experts in everything themselves.

We believe that whatever the leader's role, it can be done more effectively by using the skills and language of coaching. A leader can always become more forceful and directive, but once the leader begins there, it is much harder to revert to a collaborative and coaching mode.

3

Committed
Listening

Speech is a joint game between the talker and the listener against the forces of confusion. Unless both make the effort, interpersonal communication is quite hopeless.

—Norbert Weiner, *The Human Use of Human Beings*

While all conversations involve listeners and speakers, coaching conversations connect you more effectively with others because you intentionally focus on committed listening skills and powerful habits of speaking. By deliberately deciding to be a committed listener, you convey to the other person that they are valued, that you are open to their ideas even if you do not agree with them, and that you sincerely want to engage in a dialogue rather than a monologue. Through committed listening you are able to build relationships and trust or at least maintain a neutral stance.

In this chapter you will

- Identify your personal listening habits
- Explore the components of committed listening

- Realize how unproductive patterns of listening negatively affect interactions with others
- Discover the power of committed listening

Committed listening is foundational to all coaching conversations. When you are focused on listening to another person, you open the door to gaining clarity about issues and understanding the perceptions and needs of the other person. You also may gather more accurate data and provide space for the speaker to refine his thinking, knowing that he is really being heard. By being a committed listener, you lay the groundwork for building relationships and creating solutions to problems.

Even young children know when they are speaking with a committed listener.

When Kristin was three years old, she asked her mother to listen to a story she wished to share about her day's events. Kristin began to talk about what she had done in nursery school that day. Abruptly Kristin stopped chatting about school and exclaimed, "Mommy, you aren't listening to me!" Her mother assured her that every word had been heard, to which the young child replied, "No, you are not listening to me. I mean listening with your eyes!"

Of course Kristin's mother then realized that since she had told her daughter she would listen to her, it was vitally important to give her full attention, both mind and body to what her little girl said. After all, children, too, need committed listeners and these early conversations serve as excellent listening models for our youth as they grow into adults and enter into their own coaching conversations through committed listening.

How often have you thought you were being a good listener only to find that the other person felt unheard? For example, teenagers are notorious for saying to their parents, "You never listen to me!" What are they really saying? Perhaps "I want a voice," "I want to be reassured that you trust me," "I want you to recognize that I am my own

person—that I have my own opin-
ions, my own values, and my own
priorities."

> Committed listening
> recognizes the needs and
> values of others.

In our professional lives, people
also have these same basic needs
to have a voice, to be valued, to be recognized as individuals
who are competent and have their own set of values and priorities. Committed listening recognizes the needs and values
of others. At the same time, being a committed listener does
not mean that you agree with the speaker, or that you must
abandon your own priorities or values. Simply put, committed listening sends the message that you respect and value the
speaker. This is an important element for developing relational trust.

Listening Assessment

Effective people are aware of their personal strengths and
weaknesses. Before learning how to be a committed listener, it
is important to assess your current listening skills. This will
provide a starting point for enhancing your listening skills.
The following survey will allow you to assess your personal
listening habits. Once you complete the survey you will have
a profile of your listening habits and will be ready to develop
an action plan for making committed listening skills a personal and professional habit. Committed listening is the critical first step toward engaging in transformational coaching
conversations. See Figure 3.1.

Moving to Action

Once you have completed the listening assessment, take a few
minutes to reflect on your responses. Using the chart in Figure 3.3,
Assessment of Listening Qualities—Action Plan, write the listening qualities that you execute well, examples that demonstrate how you know you have these qualities, and the

Figure 3.1   Listening Skills Self Assessment

To help you start to be more aware of your listening habits, complete the following listening self-evaluation. It will give you an idea of which listening habits you can be happy about and which ones you might want to reshape. Answer each question thoughtfully.

Put an X in the appropriate column. Do you

		Most of the time	Frequently	Occasionally	Almost never
1.	Tune out people who say something you don't agree with or don't want to hear?				
2.	Concentrate on what is being said even if you are not really interested?				
3.	Assume you know what the talker is going to say and stop listening?				
4.	Repeat in your own words what the talker has just said?				
5.	Listen to the other person's viewpoint, even if it differs from yours?				
6.	Learn something from each person you meet, even if it is ever so slight?				
7.	Find out what words mean when they are used in ways not familiar to you?				
8.	Form a rebuttal in your head while the speaker is talking?				
9.	Give the appearance of listening when you aren't?				
10.	Daydream while the speaker is talking?				
11.	Listen to the whole message—what the talker is saying verbally and nonverbally?				
12.	Recognize that words don't mean exactly the same thing to different people?				
13.	Listen to only what you want to hear, blotting out the talker's whole message?				
14.	Look at the person who is talking?				

		Most of the time	Frequently	Occasionally	Almost never
15.	Concentrate on the talker's meaning rather than how he or she looks?				
16.	Know which words and phrases you respond to emotionally?				
17.	Think about what you want to accomplish with your communication?				
18.	Plan the best time to say what you want to say?				
19.	Think about how the other person might react to what you say?				
20.	Consider the best way to make your communication (written, spoken, phone, bulletin board, memo, etc.) work?				
21.	Think about what kind of person you're talking to (worried, hostile, disinterested, rushed, shy, stubborn, impatient, etc.)?				
22.	Interrupt the talker while he or she is still talking?				
23.	Think, "I assumed he or she would know that"?				
24.	Allow the talker to vent negative feelings toward you without becoming defensive?				
25.	Practice regularly to increase your listening efficiency?				
26.	Take notes when necessary to help you to remember?				
27.	Hear noises without being distracted by them?				
28.	Listen to the talker without judging or criticizing?				
29.	Restate instructions and messages to be sure you understand correctly?				
30.	Paraphrase what you believe the talker is feeling?				

From Madelyn Burley-Allen, *Communication Self-Assessment Evaluation*, www.dynamics-hb.com

(Continued)

(Figure 3.1 Continued)

Scoring Index: Listening Skills Self Assessment

Circle the number that matches the time frame (most of the time, frequently, etc.) you checked on each of the 30 items of the self-evaluation.
   Example: If you put an X under "frequently" for number 1, you would circle 2 in the "frequently" column.
   Then, add the circled scores in each of the columns. Now, write the scores of each column in the lines under each time frame category.

	Most of the Time	Frequently	Occasionally	Almost Never		Most of the Time	Frequently	Occasionally	Almost Never
1	1	2	3	4	16	4	3	2	1
2	4	3	2	1	17	4	3	2	1
3	1	2	3	4	18	4	3	2	1
4	4	3	2	1	19	4	3	2	1
5	4	3	2	1	20	4	3	2	1
6	4	3	2	1	21	4	3	2	1
7	4	3	2	1	22	1	2	3	4
8	1	2	3	4	23	1	2	3	4
9	1	2	3	4	24	4	3	2	1
10	1	2	3	4	25	4	3	2	1
11	4	3	2	1	26	4	3	2	1
12	4	3	2	1	27	4	3	2	1
13	1	2	3	4	28	4	3	2	1
14	4	3	2	1	29	4	3	2	1
15	4	3	2	1	30	4	3	2	1
Totals					Totals				

Total of items circled in each column:

	Most of the Time	Frequently	Occasionally	Almost Never	Total
Grand Totals	_____ +	_____ +	_____ +	_____ =	_____

Scoring

110–120	Superior	_____
99–109	Above Average	_____
88–98	Average	_____
77–87	Fair	_____

From Madelyn Burley-Allen, Communication Self-Assessment Evaluation www.dynamics-hb.com

Figure 3.2   Assessment of Listening Qualities—Action Plan Sample

Listening Qualities I Have	How I Know
I am expert at observing body language.	I focus on maintaining eye contact when people speak to me and recognize when their words do not match their tone of voice and facial expressions.
Listening Qualities I Want to Develop	
I want to become a more committed listener by tuning into what others say, even when I do not agree with them.	

© Coaching For Results, Inc. (2007)

Figure 3.3   Assessment of Listening Qualities—Action Plan

Listening Qualities I Have	How I Know
Listening Qualities I Want to Develop	

© Coaching For Results, Inc. (2007)

listening qualities you want to develop. Figure 3.2 provides a sample chart. If you are an expert on observing body language, list this quality under *listening qualities I have*. You may know that you have this skill because you focus on maintaining eye contact with the speaker. You would write this observation under *how I know*. If you want to become a more committed listener by tuning into what others say, even when you do not agree with them, write this in the block labeled *listening qualities I want to develop*. Frequently reviewing and revising this chart will help you learn and grow effective listening skills.

Components of Committed Listening

When you are a committed listener (see Figure 3.4) you focus your full attention—mind and body—on what the other person is saying. You listen not only to the words expressed but also to underlying emotions and body language. In other words you listen to the *essence* of the conversation. Committed listeners also recognize the value of silence in conversations and avoid unproductive listening patterns that interfere with the deep listening of coaching conversations.

Moreover committed listeners recognize that sometimes the speaker just needs us to listen—to hear what they are saying. If you are engaged in committed listening, you will know if the other person wants information, a response, or just to be heard. According to Dennis Sparks (2007), "Committed listening transforms relationships and deepens learning. Its skillful use requires practice and discipline" (p. 71).

Verbal and Nonverbal Communication

Nearly two-thirds of meaning between speakers comes from nonverbal cues—what we see in the speaker's face and body, and what we hear in the voice tone.

How often have you listened to staff members and although their words said one thing, you knew their messages to you were very different? We all know that adage, "Actions speak louder than words." Nearly two-thirds of meaning between speakers comes from nonverbal cues—what we see in the speaker's face and body, and what we hear in the voice tone. So your nonverbal communication has *more* impact on others than the words you speak. It is very important that your body language and other nonverbal cues align with the message you want to convey. Conversely by listening to others in a committed manner, you will "hear" the full message being conveyed to you.

Figure 3.4 Components of Committed Listening

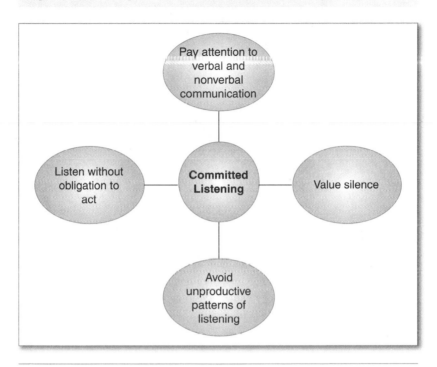

Adapted from Coaching For Results, Inc. (2007)

For example, a teacher has just told you that she would be happy to serve on the school's new data analysis committee. Yet you can tell by the tightening of her jaw and the tone of her voice that she is not at all "happy" about the new assignment. As a committed listener you would notice the disconnect between her words and her physical responses. You would know that it was time for a coaching conversation. Let's examine another example in which nonverbal cues did not align with the intended message:

Suzette, a middle school English teacher, was at the end of a long day of parent conferences. She was tired, hungry, and had a pounding headache. Her last conference was with the Mitchell family. Joey Mitchell was a quiet student, getting average grades, and Suzette was glad that she could end the day with a quick and easy conference.

> *So the next day Suzette was very surprised to learn that Joey's parents had complained to the principal about her. "She frowned the whole time and had very little to say about our son," they said. "We don't think she likes him and we are not sure we want him to continue in her class."*

Suzette's body language had conveyed a completely different message to the parents than she had intended.

> *In a follow-up coaching conversation the principal asked Suzette what she would like to do about the situation. Suzette listed a number of strategies she could use and they agreed on her response to the parents.*
>
> *Then the principal asked her what she had learned from this experience that would be helpful to her in the future. Suzette immediately identified the importance of watching her body language during her parent conferences. She responded, "If I want to convey that I am a caring teacher, I must watch my voice tone and enthusiasm level. I should give as much time to the last conference as to the first."*
>
> *She vowed to pay close attention to the spirit she wanted to convey in her future parent conferences as well as the message.*

Monitoring the alignment between the words you hear and the nonverbal language and behaviors of those with whom you interact provides important cues as you develop committed listening skills.

Value Silence

In the United States people rarely seek silence. Instead our days are filled with chatter, e-mail, twitters, texting, telephone conversations, music, TV and other noisy interactions and distracters. In social situations our habit is to immediately fill any gaps in conversation. Yet in the classroom we expect our teachers to provide "wait time" after they ask questions of their students. Research has long demonstrated the value of wait time. More students will respond, their replies will often involve higher order thinking skills, and children will have time to process information better. We value silence in our classrooms.

Imagine if you also valued silence during your daily conversations. What might result? When you focus on providing the speakers with space and time for reflection and processing, you gift them with committed listening.

Margaret, the beloved high school math teacher, had asked to speak to Superintendent Robert. When she entered his office she began crying. Robert checked to be sure that the tissue box was in sight but did not directly offer it. He simply helped Margaret sit down and then sat beside her, putting his hand gently on her arm. "It's OK," he said. "Whenever you are ready to talk, I am here." And then he was quiet.

After a few moments, Margaret composed herself and uttered, "I have just learned that I have Stage 2 leukemia. My doctor says I must begin treatment right away."

Again, Robert waited, simply listening for her to continue. After a pause Margaret continued, "Surgery is scheduled for next week and then chemotherapy." Another pause. "I won't be able to end the school year as I had hoped and I don't even know about teaching next year." Then Margaret cried again.

Robert gave her a minute to regroup and then offered a tissue. "This is really tough news. . . . Don't worry about this year or next. . . . Concentrate on getting yourself well," he stated.

Finally Robert asked, "So what can I do to help?"

Margaret responded by asking him questions about sick leave, long-term substitutes, and other school-related issues.

Because of Robert's wise use of silence, Margaret was able to tell the superintendent emotionally laden information and given time to get to the root of what was really worrying her. He provided "sacred space" for her to talk and his silence allowed her to control the timing, pace, and direction of a conversation that was very difficult for her.

Unproductive Patterns of Listening

Committed listeners are effective because they focus their energy on the other person's verbal and nonverbal communication and they value silence. This deep level of listening requires practice in avoiding unproductive listening patterns. Imagine how differently the conversation between Robert and Margaret might have ended if the superintendent had immediately started giving advice to Margaret or talked about a serious illness in his own family. She probably would not have felt supported and may have left Robert's office feeling more upset than when she entered. Later Margaret might even have shared with her teaching colleagues her negative experience in Robert's office. In this alternate scenario, surely the trust level between the superintendent and his staff would have been harmed.

Ineffective conversations often result when people engage in four unproductive patterns of listening:

1. Judgment or criticism

2. Autobiographical listening

3. Inquisitive listening

4. Solution listening

1. Judgment or Criticism

Judgment or criticism occurs when the listener focuses attention on hearing flaws in what is being said, hoping to discredit the speaker or setting up an adversarial relationship with the other person. Often the listener has an opposing viewpoint. As a result:

- Criticism becomes not only the first step in the conversation; it often is the last step, too, shutting down the possibility for discussion to take place.
- Judgment sends the message that only one person has the "right" answers.

- When you attack ideas you reduce the possibility for creative thinking and problem solving to occur.
- Criticism may be the way some people are able to influence others.
- Judgment conditions others to be dependent on us for approval, leading to a loss of self-confidence and a breakdown in trust.

Response examples of judgment or criticism include:

- "Why did you do it that way?"
- "You explained your ideas poorly."
- "I tried that last week and it didn't work."
- "I really like Gerry's plan." (When you approve one plan, all others are discredited.)

The next vignette demonstrates how judgment or criticism has impacted a school leader in a negative way:

Principal George had been urged by his assistant superintendent to practice shared leadership with his staff. He decided to involve his teachers in problem solving an issue of student tardiness that had been impacting classroom discipline. At a staff meeting he invited his faculty to suggest new and creative ways to address this schoolwide problem. Yet as the staff members offered alternatives and solution ideas, George gave a reason why each idea would not work.

1. He had already thought of that strategy but dismissed it because . . .

2. That solution was tried before but did not work

3. The idea would be too hard to implement

The staff quickly stopped offering input because George was dismissing their ideas without really listening to the possibilities suggested. George was frustrated because so few staff seemed interested in offering good ideas.

In a follow-up session with his coach, George discussed his frustration with his attempt to involve staff in solving the tardiness issue.

> The coach responded, "You have identified this discipline issue as a good way to share some decision making with your staff and you are disappointed that they did not give you any good ideas. From your experience, what are the key criteria for a good solution?"
>
> George thought a minute and then replied, "Well, the idea would need to be relatively easy to implement. . . . It would need to connect with the students. . . . And I want the solution to focus on the positive, not on more punitive measures."
>
> "Good!" replied the coach. "Now what are some ways you could ask the staff to think about these criteria when they are offering their ideas?"
>
> After reflecting for a moment, George responded, "I could ask staff members to offer ideas, giving the pros, cons, and interesting facts related to these criteria. Would that work?"
>
> "That sounds like a brilliant idea!" said the coach. "It would give the staff input into the solution while at the same time allow them to use your experience as a frame of reference."

By developing and communicating his selection criteria from the beginning, George was able to share leadership as well as give staff the benefit of his experience. After George reframed his request for ideas from the staff, new solution ideas emerged and a good one was selected to try schoolwide.

As you meet with members of your own school community, consider how you receive their thoughts. How open are you to considering the ideas they suggest? How often do you encourage discussion without criticism? In what ways could you enhance conversations by being committed to listening without judgment?

2. Autobiographical Listening

Autobiographical listening is another unproductive pattern of listening. It is also called "piggybacking" or "highjacking" a conversation. One person discusses an activity or idea that stimulates the associative power of the listener's brain to think of his own similar experience. His attention may wander, he may compare himself with the speaker, or he may be eager to respond with his own story. Committed listeners refrain from telling their own stories and focus their full attention on just listening to the speaker.

Think of a theater production. The spotlight shines on the actor who is speaking. If another character then enters the stage and begins to speak, the spotlight moves away from the former speaker and now shines on the new actor. Piggybacking in a conversation turns the spotlight off the speaker and onto the listener. When you are fully committed to listening to the original speaker rather than your own inner voice, you keep the spotlight focused on the speaker rather than on yourself.

Juanita entered the teachers' lunch room and began a conversation with another third-grade teacher named Gary. Juanita expressed her concern about a child in her class who rarely interacted with the other children. This student only wanted to talk with the teacher and sought her attention constantly.

Before Juanita could say another word, Gary expressed that he had dealt with the exact same problem last year. Gary then went on to describe his former student's behavior in great detail and how he had handled the problem. Juanita quickly realized that Gary was really not interested in listening to her story and she resolved to refrain from talking about her concerns with Gary again.

Gary may have thought he was establishing rapport and showing sympathy when he told Juanita his story, but he was really driving her away. What might have been the outcome of this conversation if Gary had been a committed listener instead of piggybacking on Juanita's story? Let's revisit the conversation:

After Juanita entered the teachers' lunch room and began her conversation with him, Gary intentionally focused on not just the words that Juanita expressed but also her underlying emotions and unstated values that students should feel comfortable with their peers and grow less dependent on the teacher as the school year progressed.

Throughout the conversation, Gary gave Juanita his full attention. He asked a few clarifying questions and occasionally paraphrased what Juanita said so that she might reflect on her concerns.

At the end of the conversation, Juanita asked Gary what she should do. Instead of telling her how he had handled this situation in his own teaching experience, he asked Juanita what she would like to do and helped her generate a list of 10 possible solutions.

Juanita left the conversation feeling that Gary had really heard and understood her. Moreover, she was now confident that she could solve this dilemma herself, recognizing that several of the ideas she had generated with Gary's encouragement were strong possibilities for helping her student. In addition she learned that she could count on Gary's support in the future.

Consider your conversations. What happens when you highjack another person's story? How does that differ from when you listen to someone in a committed manner without interjecting your own story? What actions might you take to ensure that you are a committed listener who keeps the conversational spotlight on other people?

3. Inquisitive Listening

A third unproductive pattern of listening results when people become overly curious about irrelevant portions of the speaker's story. Instead of listening to the essence of the other person's message, they become curious about irrelevant details of the story. Consider this example:

Jack, a high school assistant principal, was talking to a colleague, Celia, about a very difficult phone call he had had with a parent. Jack wanted Celia to understand that he was angry and needed to express his negative emotions in a safe manner. Instead Celia interrupted Jack with a number of specific questions about his story, such as "What time did the parent call?" and "Who teaches that student?" Jack quickly sensed that his colleague was not really listening to him because the conversation had bogged down in minutiae unrelated to the larger issue of his feelings. Jack left the conversation feeling unheard, frustrated, and still full of the emotions he had felt during his phone call with the parent.

In a coaching conversation Celia would have listened fully to her colleague by focusing her complete attention on both the words and underlying emotions that Jack was expressing. Instead of asking for irrelevant data, Celia would have recognized that Jack just needed someone to listen to him. All that Jack had asked of her was to be a trusted and committed listener. If Celia had just listened to her colleague without any obligation to question or respond, Jack might have left the conversation feeling free of his negative emotions and more ready to face the rest of his day with a more positive outlook.

4. Solution Listening

A fourth unproductive pattern of listening is *solution listening*. When someone shares a problem with school leaders, they are often eager to provide a quick and helpful solution—even when the other person has not asked for their advice! After all, many school administrators are promoted to their leadership positions because they are such good problem solvers. However, solution listening may lead you to filter your thinking as you focus on the parts of the conversation that support your solution and not the entire conversation. As the other person speaks, you may even be rehearsing how you will present your solution!

Marcus was teaching poetry to an eighth-grade class. He was frustrated because the students seemed so disinterested and unengaged. He had an idea to use musical lyrics as a connection for motivating the students but wanted to share his thoughts with his principal, Rosa, first. "I have been really frustrated with the behavior of my students recently. We are doing a poetry unit and they aren't paying attention and won't

*do their homework. And this is a tested area on the state
assessments!" Marcus said in an exasperated manner.*

*Rosa replied, "Have you thought about using cooperative learning
groups? Or what about creating some new incentives that the
students really like? Or maybe I can come in and talk to them—you
know, lay down the law and remind them that if they don't straighten
up they won't get to go on the upcoming field trip."*

*Marcus left the principal's office feeling disappointed and
frustrated. He really wanted to share his teaching idea with the
principal but she jumped to solution thinking too soon. So he
received discipline ideas from Rosa and left without knowing if she
would support his new teaching strategy.*

Conversely, an effective committed listener focuses on
understanding the speaker's perspective. A coaching conversation between Marcus and his principal might have ended
very differently if Rosa had refrained from providing solutions and just listened to her teacher.

*After listening to Marcus discuss his frustration about teaching
unmotivated learners, Rosa replied, "I can hear the disappointment in
your voice, Marcus." She continued, "What are you thinking of doing?"*

*Then Marcus proceeded to tell her his idea about integrating
lyrics from popular music into his poetry unit. Rosa asked several
more questions about the idea, including the criteria Marcus would
use to select the music and what his evidence of success would be.
After a short conversation, Marcus left Rosa's office confident that
she would support his new teaching plan, and Rosa knew she
would get an update on the project from Marcus within two weeks.*

Listen Without Obligation to Act

When others share with us, they are not automatically asking
us for a response. If your colleague tells you that she wants to
move to a new house, you do not immediately call a real
estate agent for her. She may just want to discuss her needs,

sort out her desires, and explore possibilities. Sometimes you just need to listen without any obligation to act. For example:

After one particular coaching session, Dorice, a district director of special education, had committed to practice listening without obligation to act. Later that same day, an angry parent, Mr. Landry, demanded to speak immediately with the director about a lunch aide's treatment of his son on the playground. Dorice remembered her commitment to listening fully and invited the father to tell her why he was so upset. Dorice sat in a chair directly across from the parent instead of her usual practice of sitting behind her desk. She nodded as Mr. Landry spoke and kept her mind open to what he said.

For the next 15 minutes, Dorice said nothing except to ask the father a few clarifying questions so that she was sure she understood the problem fully. She refrained from asking the parent for unnecessary details. When it became clear that the parent had finished telling his story, Dorice carefully avoided criticizing him, defending the school aide, or telling the father what would happen next. Instead, after a few moments of silence, Dorice simply asked the father what his expectations were for what should happen next. To her great surprise, Mr. Landry thought for a moment and then responded, "Actually, I don't really want anything more to happen. I was angry, you listened to me, and now that I feel heard, I realize that's all I needed."

Dorice had experienced and learned the power of listening without obligation to act.

In what ways could you apply the concept of listening without obligation to respond to your school leadership conversations? How might this change your school's culture? In what ways might interactions with staff, students, and parents be different?

A psychologist shared one of his most valuable strategies with one of our colleagues. He disclosed that frequently people come to us irrationally thinking they want us to fix or do something immediately. In their hearts they know that we probably cannot solve the problem or give them what they want. Instead there is one thing they do consciously expect—that the person with whom they speak will see their passion, recognize their frustration, or empathize with their concerns.

Our coaching colleague, Kathy Kee, has coined a phrase for this way of listening. She calls it "witnessing the struggle." By your presence and committed listening, you convey that you empathize with the speaker. Listening without any obligation to act allows you to hear what the other person is saying rather than formulating your next response. You are willing to *witness the struggle*.

> Listening without any obligation to act allows you to hear what the other person is saying rather than formulating your next response.

Summary

Committed listening is foundational to all coaching conversations. It allows you to gain clarity on issues and understand the needs and perceptions of others, helps you gather data more completely and accurately, and encourages others to think more deeply. Through committed listening, you provide opportunities for building trust with others and create space for new solutions.

A committed listener tunes into numerous verbal and nonverbal cues to understand the *essence* of what is said rather than the exact words spoken. Committed listeners recognize the value of silence in a conversation. Moments of silence provide the speaker with opportunities to reflect and dig deeper, allowing them to express their thoughts more accurately and fully.

Effective, committed listening requires both an understanding of your own listening skills and dedicated practice so that you may avoid unproductive listening patterns, such as judgmental, autobiographical, inquisitive and solution listening.

In addition, a committed listener recognizes the power of just listening, without any obligation to act upon what is said. Coaching conversations emphasize committed listening that builds the relationship with the speaker in an honest and authentic manner.

4

Powerful Speaking

To speak and to speak well are two things. A fool may talk, but a wise man speaks.

—Ben Jonson

It was impossible to get a conversation going; everybody was talking too much.

—Yogi Berra

Coaching conversations that build relationships, lead to deeper thinking and result in long-term change involve both committed listening and connecting powerfully through very intentional speaking skills.

Many of your daily speech patterns would be more effective in helping you to achieve your goals and engage in coaching conversations if you were very intentional about the purpose for your conversations and if you used language that clearly expresses and aligns with your inner thoughts.

In this chapter you will learn how to recognize and apply powerful language through

- Creating an intention for conversations
- Choosing words at the appropriate level
- Forming positive presuppositions
- Valuing the importance of avoiding advice
- Understanding and developing powerful questions

Connecting powerfully through speaking allows you to align your thinking with your words and provides a safe environment for others to listen to what you are saying. When you speak powerfully you intentionally focus on specific goals for the conversation and then choose words that will support your goals. In addition, powerful speakers recognize how important it is to avoid giving advice. They form positive presuppositions about others and they incorporate powerful questions into their conversations. See Figure 4.1.

> Powerful speaking is about having a positive influence on others.

By learning and practicing each of the steps outlined below, you will be able to speak powerfully as you hold coaching conversations with members of your school community. It is important to recognize that speaking powerfully is about the personal connections you make to others with whom you are speaking. Powerful speaking is about having a positive influence on others and is the antithesis of autocratic or authoritarian demands by one person on other people.

Create an Intention

When engaged in a coaching conversation, a powerful speaker recognizes the importance of creating her intention before talking. In other words she first considers the goal of the conversation. This is a process that takes place in one's mind before a single word is uttered. For example, a school leader may have an intention to support a staff member, create an opportunity for reflective thinking, challenge ideas, or share the vision for

Figure 4.1   Speaking Powerfully

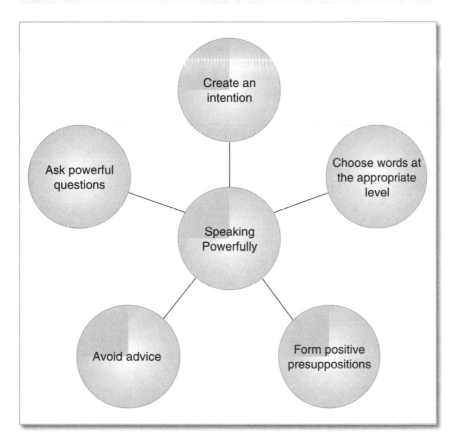

Adapted from Coaching For Results, Inc. (2007)

the school. Only after a school leader has established the intention for the conversation will her attention now be focused and she will be ready to move to action—to express herself so that her words are aligned with what she wants to say.

Often leaders move to action or speak too quickly because they have not thought through their intention or their goal for talking and then focused their attention on this conversational objective. Simply put, they speak without thinking.

Imagine a cannon is about to be fired. The person in charge yells, "Ready. *Fire.* Aim."

How often would the target be hit? In this situation you recognize that the correct sequence should be, "Ready. *Aim.* Fire." Of course the cannon must first be readied with ammunition and then aimed at the target before orders are given to fire the cannon!

Yet how often do leaders talk first and then think about why they are speaking—if they think at all about the purpose for the conversation?

Even when they have a goal in mind for a conversation, most people, including school leaders, frequently move directly from the intention—the goal—to action without considering how they want "to be" in the conversation, that is, first figuring out the context for the message. Powerful speakers get *ready* (form an intention for the content of the message), *aim* (think about the context of the message), and then *fire* (take action by speaking to achieve the intention).

Matt is the principal of a large, urban middle school and one of his eighth-grade mathematics teachers, Yvonne, has fallen into the habit of loosely preparing her lessons by just working page by page through the textbook with her students. However the school has a clearly articulated vision that focuses on each student's growth and achievement through differentiated instruction. Matt decided that it was time to have a coaching conversation with Yvonne. Before meeting with her, he took time to reflect on his goal for the conversation, the kinds of open-ended questions he might ask the teacher, the tone he wanted to project, and how he would frame his expectations.

His initial reflection caused Matt to wonder why Yvonne had fallen into the habit of just teaching from the book. He decided to enter the conversation with a positive presupposition that Yvonne wanted to serve her students well. She may just have needed a fuller understanding of differentiated instructional practices and more support from her colleagues as good teaching role models.

Once Matt had a clear intention for his conversation with Yvonne and was well-prepared for a powerful coaching conversation with the teacher, he was then ready to move forward and schedule a time to meet with Yvonne.

Even if a school leader intends to hold a supervisory conversation, his words should reflect a specific, intentional goal. In this case, Matt would have prepared for his conversation with Yvonne by clarifying in his mind the goals or outcomes he wanted to achieve, and determining what was or was not negotiable. For example, in Matt's school, implementing differentiated instructional practices was non-negotiable—all teachers were expected to implement strategies that would assist every student achieve at high levels. As he reflected about his pending supervisory conversation with Yvonne, Matt was open-minded about the process and recognized that he wanted to gain clarity as to why she had not implemented the required instructional processes and that this information could inform him as to next steps. The format of the remedial plan was negotiable. In the end, though, he was very intentional that in his supervisory conversation, Yvonne would be required to follow a clear remedial plan that would result in her implementation of differentiated instructional techniques.

In this example of a supervisory conversation, Matt was still very intentional regarding his goals and what was non-negotiable. At the same time, he remained open-minded about why Yvonne was not using the expected instructional techniques and he was willing to negotiate specific steps for remediating the problem.

Although a supervisory conversation is directive in nature, as Matt's story illustrates, it is still possible to incorporate elements from coaching conversations into the process.

Choose Words at the Appropriate Level

After powerful speakers create an intention for speaking, they choose very specific language that aligns their intentions with their goals. If you listen to the words you use to tell your stories, describe your goals, and express your ideas, you may be surprised how often you use words that do not express your thoughts clearly to others. For example, you may use the language of obligation—"I *have to* work with my teachers to

raise academic standards in our school for all students."
Expressing your goals to others, however, requires the language of commitment or promise. "I am *committed to* work with my staff to do whatever it takes to raise the academic standards in our school for all students." Telling other people that you *have* to, *need* to, or *should* take an action is vastly different from saying that you are *committed* to or *intend* to follow through on a plan of action.

Failure to keep commitments erodes trust and relationships.

On the other hand very few statements should be made at the commitment or *promise* level of speaking. It is far better to under promise and over deliver than to use the language of commitment and then fail to keep that promise. Failure to keep commitments erodes trust and relationships.

A visionary leader monitors his use of obligatory language. Frequent use of "I have to," "I should," "I must," or "I need to" sends the message that the speaker considers most activities strictly as chores and obligations. Listeners may become unmotivated or feel that their work is not valued by the school leader.

By choosing the level of your language with intention, you align your speech with your inner purpose and goals. Dave Ellis in *Falling Awake* (2000) uses the metaphor of a ladder to analyze speech patterns. See Figure 4.2.

Each step of the ladder represents a different level of intention in our speech. The bottom step is the level of *obligation* and the top rung is the level of *promise* or *commitment*. There is no value judgment about one step on the ladder being better than another. Instead what is important is to match your inner intentions with words that accurately express what you mean to convey to others. *Promising* a friend that you will meet him at noon for lunch is a commitment that means you will definitely show up for the luncheon at noon sharp. If in your mind, you know you may be delayed until 12:30 PM, then your friend may end up being angry with you because you "promised" to arrive at noon. To avoid this possible outcome and build the relationship with your friend, it is

Figure 4.2   Ladder of Intentional Speech Patterns

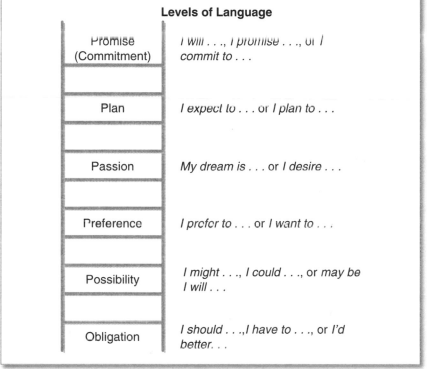

Levels of Language	
Promise (Commitment)	*I will . . ., I promise . . ., or I commit to . . .*
Plan	*I expect to . . . or I plan to . . .*
Passion	*My dream is . . . or I desire . . .*
Preference	*I prefer to . . . or I want to . . .*
Possibility	*I might . . ., I could . . ., or may be I will . . .*
Obligation	*I should . . .,I have to . . ., or I'd better. . .*

Adapted from Dave Ellis (2000), *Falling Awake*

important to align your words with your intention. In this example you might say, "I *plan* to arrive at noon, and I want you to know that I have an earlier meeting that may run late, so I may arrive as late as 12:30 PM. Is this OK with you?" Now, your friend can choose to wait for you or set another time to get together. Your words have conveyed that you want to eat with your friend and that you also value his time and respect his judgment in deciding whether or not to keep the current luncheon date.

Imagine a couple about to exchange vows at their wedding. You would expect that they would speak of their commitment to each other. Their words would be at the level of *promise*. Consider the impact of language if their words were at any level below that of *promise*.

Promise: "I commit myself to being faithful to you for our lifetime." (No matter what happens!)

Plan: "I plan to be faithful to you." (And sometimes plans change.)

Passion: "I'm wild about you and want to spend every waking moment with you." (This level of intense feeling may not be able to be sustained over time and it might make me feel restricted.)

Preference: "I want to be faithful to you." (At this moment, this is what I want. I might decide I prefer something else later.)

Possibility: "I might be faithful to you." (Then again, I might not.)

Obligation: "I know I have to be faithful to you." (Being married is a real burden.)

A wedding is the perfect time to use language at the level of *promise*. In your daily life, however, it is better to under commit and over deliver rather than the reverse. When you use the promise level of language you are creating an informal contract with the listener. As a school leader if you promise to provide a teacher with all of the materials she needs to work with a student in her class who has special needs, she has a right to believe that you will keep that promise. Consider another example:

Alex had been the science supervisor of his school for five years when one of his experienced teachers, Danielle Jacobs, left a note in his mailbox. He was surprised to read, "This is a reminder that you promised to visit my classroom this afternoon at 2 PM to hear my students make their group presentations for science."

Later that day, Alex asked Danielle why she had sent him the note because she knew that he had listed the event on his calendar for the day. The teacher responded, "You have promised to visit my class many times but you frequently do not show up. Even though you have good reasons for not coming, my students are disappointed when they expect to see you and then you miss their events."

Alex realized that he had used the word *promise* when a different level of language would have been more accurate, such as "I plan to visit" or "I might be able to visit your class." The teacher and her class would then know that the supervisor was interested in visiting them, yet he might not be able to come if other priorities took precedence on his time. It is always better to under promise and then over deliver!

School leaders who speak powerfully also avoid overusing obligatory language—"I should be in the classrooms more," "I have to observe three teachers today," "I have to hold a meeting with the parent association tomorrow."

Jennifer is a coaching client who serves as the lead reading/language arts teacher in her elementary school. During one coaching session, she described how teachers rarely asked her for assistance this year. This was in stark contrast to prior school years when teachers frequently sought her help and invited her to visit their classes.

When asked what she thought might be the reason for this change in her relationships with the other teachers, Jennifer indicated that she had been put in charge of the school's testing program this year and also had many more written reports to complete for a variety of funded programs.

When coached to figure out what connections these extra duties might have to her declining interactions with staff, Jennifer recognized that when teachers approached her for help this year, she often expressed how stressed she was about all of the extra work she had to do. Jennifer realized that staff may have avoided requests for help and invitations because they did not want to trouble her with more work.

Once Jennifer understood how negatively her words had impacted the most rewarding part of her position, she developed a plan for scheduling more time to work with teachers and students in classrooms and made a commitment to herself to monitor her language when speaking with staff.

Through reflection Jennifer grasped that she could allocate her time more efficiently, which would provide her with additional time for direct contact with teachers and students. She made a personal commitment to avoid obligatory language during her conversations with staff. She also learned to change her inner language and view her latest job responsibilities as additional means for helping the teachers and students in her school rather than as extra burdens. By choosing the level of her words with intention Jennifer found renewed joy in all aspects of her professional activities.

Positive Presuppositions: Expressing Positive Intent

Meaning is always embedded in language even if the meaning does not emerge from the actual structure of the sentences you speak. By paying attention to the words you choose, you may positively or negatively influence the feelings and thinking of others with whom you are communicating. As soon as you speak your words convey either a positive or negative intention to the listener.

Consider the following examples:

Do you have any objectives for today's lesson?	versus	What objectives have you developed for today's lesson?
Have you thought about your meeting with Joe's parents?	versus	What options are you considering for your meeting with Joe's parents?
Did you finish the agenda for today's staff meeting?	versus	What goals have you set for today's staff meeting?
Will the report be done by Friday?	versus	As a conscientious school leader, what methods are you using to gather the information you need for Friday's report?
Are your students ready for the state tests?	versus	As a teacher who always puts his students first, what strategies are you considering to ensure their success on the state tests?

What do you notice about each of the questions? What feelings might the language in the questions on the left evoke versus the questions on the right? In what ways do the questions on the right differ from those on the left? What are the intentions for each question?

Negative language is everywhere in school environments, such as "Have you thought about how much your suggestion will cost?" "Did you check references before you hired the new teaching assistant?" "Even a substitute teacher could have figured that out!" Questions that begin with *did you* or *have you* require, at best, a one word response: *yes* or *no*. These close-ended questions and negative remarks may also cause the listener to feel defensive, frustrated, inadequate, and dependent.

Yet when educators learn to use positive language they communicate the standard(s) to be met while affirming efforts and skills. Coaching conversations focus on positive language that provides opportunities for reflective thinking, generation of solutions, and relationship building between speakers and listeners. If you enter conversations with the positive intent that those with whom you speak are competent, dedicated, and want to have a constructive influence on the world, the other person is much more likely to hear your message and respond in a positive, or at least neutral, manner.

Visionary school leaders rarely intend to deliver negative messages. However they have learned ineffective speech patterns that foster negative results. As with the other skills that lead to effective coaching conversations, deliberately creating and practicing positive presuppositions about those with whom you interact may result in rich opportunities for discussion, cooperation, and growth.

Use Figure 4.3 to practice transforming negative language into statements and questions that reflect positive intent. Rewrite each question on the left so that it conveys a positive presupposition.

Figure 4.3   Practicing Positive Intentions

Negative Intentions	Versus	Positive Intentions
Why didn't you help Frank with that problem?	versus	
Have you been using running records?	versus	
Are you prepared for the principal's observation?	versus	
Do you know any good writing topics?	versus	
Did you hand in your grade reports?	versus	
Have you developed differentiated instruction plans for your students?	versus	
You are late for the meeting. Don't you check your watch?	versus	
Are you excited about starting the new school year?	versus	

Consider the effects of forming positive presuppositions in the following example:

Gina is an assistant principal who found post observation conferences with her teachers very difficult. She wanted to acknowledge and reinforce the many wonderful teaching strategies they utilized. She knew that the conferences were also important opportunities for professional growth and development, yet teachers seemed to shut down when she asked questions about their lessons or made suggestions for improvement.

When her coach encouraged Gina to think about the kinds of questions and recommendations she used, Gina responded, "Oh the typical—Did you achieve the objectives for your lesson? Did you notice if the students were actively engaged in the lesson? You should use more 'wait time' before calling on students to answer questions."

Her coach paraphrased what Gina had said and then asked her what she noticed about her language. Gina had an aha moment when she realized that all of her questions required only yes or no responses and that her recommendations for improvement were statements that failed to provide the teachers with opportunities for reflection. Gina acknowledged that her language habits were negative. No wonder that her post observation conversations with the teachers were so unproductive!

Once Gina recognized the power of forming positive presuppositions by expressing positive intent in her language, she was eager to develop strategies for future meetings. As a start Gina created a set of generic positive questions and statements she could use in her post observation conferences. She decided that she would then think about and adjust her list of positive intentions to fit the individual needs of each teacher with whom she was conferencing. Through dedicated practice Gina noticed that positivity became a language habit for her. She also noticed that her post observation conferences had become real dialogues with teachers about best educational practices.

Forming positive presuppositions will become a language habit through practice. At first, you will begin to notice the language you use and that of others. Soon you will find yourself replacing something you were about to say with words that reflect positive intent. You may wish to begin your practice at home with family and friends. Over time you will discover many opportunities to use this powerful communication tool.

Avoid Advice

Boards of education hire school leadership candidates who demonstrate the ability to make good decisions that are grounded in best educational practices. Staff members, students, parents, and community members look to their school leaders for direction and support. These constituents learn to value the wisdom of their leaders.

Unfortunately, because a school leader often demonstrates excellent problem-solving skills, staff and others may become dependent on the leader to provide solutions and answers even when many issues could and should be handled at a lower level. In *The One Minute Manager Meets the Monkey*, Kenneth Blanchard, William Oncken Jr., and Hal Burrows (1989) use the metaphor of monkeys to demonstrate the issue of the leader taking on the problems of others. The following story illustrates how educational leaders often adopt and carry other people's *monkeys*.

Jackie, the principal of a local high school, walked daily through the halls of her school. Along the way several teachers stopped her to discuss a variety of problems and issues (their monkeys). An English teacher told Jackie that he had received an e-mail from an angry parent. Jackie promised to call the parent later in the day. A biology teacher related that many students were late in completing their science fair projects. Jackie told her what strategies to use to motivate the students to complete their work in a timely manner. The head of the mathematics department wanted to talk about problems with scheduling classes for the next year. Jackie informed him that she would look into the scheduling issue with the guidance department.

By the end of her walk-through of the building, Jackie had accumulated numerous monkeys on her back and then spent much of the remainder of the day feeding and taking care of the monkeys she had acquired.

Jackie picked up the problem monkeys that others could have handled and she reinforced to her staff that she wanted them to come to her for solutions even when they could and should have tackled their own issues. Although her intention was to help and support her staff, Jackie took action and gave advice before she thought about how she could have turned their issues into opportunities for her staff to grow more confident and learn strategies for generating their own solutions.

Solving the problems of others and giving advice are toxic! Essentially the message you send when you give direct advice or solve problems that do not belong to you is that others are not as capable as you are in resolving their issues and that they should be dependent on you as their leader because you know what is best.

In coaching conversations, instead of giving advice, the school leader supports her staff by paraphrasing what is said and asking powerful, open-ended questions that lead to deeper thinking.

Coaching conversations encourage others to be reflective and exercise responsibility. The message you send when you speak powerfully by avoiding advice is "I trust you, I support you, and it is okay to take risks."

> Coaching conversations encourage others to be reflective and exercise responsibility.

How is it possible to avoid giving advice, especially when others approach you expecting to be given a solution to a problem or when you perceive that a problem exists? Blanchard and colleagues express the leader's role this way, "Practice hands-off management as much as possible and hands-on management as much as necessary" (1989, p. 82). Listening to staff members, helping them reflect on issues, and encouraging them to generate workable solutions may be time intensive, yet it is far less time consuming in the long run to hold these coaching conversations that lead to other people taking responsibility for their own issues than to spend much of each day solving problems that could be handled more efficiently and even more effectively by others.

A recent coaching client felt overwhelmed until she realized that giving advice to her staff was a root cause for her feelings:

Cindy was a highly conscientious principal of a kindergarten through eighth-grade school. She set an ambitious goal to be in classrooms an average of 50% of each school day. During one coaching session she expressed frustration about spending so much time in her office solving problems and making decisions that kept her from being in classrooms more often.

Through reflection and enumeration of the kinds of issues that were occupying her time, Cindy realized that she had actually trained her staff to receive her approval and permission before

> *embarking on even simple and routine tasks. For example, she*
> *expected the school's head custodian to meet with her every time*
> *basic paper supplies needed to be ordered.*

Once Cindy recognized that many decisions and issues in the school required very little, if any, input from her, she was able to develop an action plan that indicated the information she always wanted to know and the kinds of decisions and information that others could handle on their own. Cindy also developed strategies to share her plan with her staff so that she would still send them the message that she cared about them and was there to help when needed. For example:

> *When Dominic Lombardi, a sixth-grade teacher approached Cindy*
> *and asked her how to deal with several girls in the class who were*
> *teasing another child, the principal avoided giving advice by asking,*
> *"What have you done so far to handle this problem?" Although the*
> *teacher had tried several strategies, he still had not solved the*
> *problem completely. Cindy then asked Dominic, "What else could*
> *you try?" By gently asking and rephrasing this same question, Cindy*
> *helped the teacher develop a list of 10 possible solutions and by the*
> *end of their meeting, Dominic had chosen two priorities for*
> *implementation. At the end of the coaching conversation, Cindy*
> *expressed her confidence in the teacher and indicated that she*
> *would stop by his classroom the following Tuesday to ask the teacher*
> *how well his strategies were working.*

Cindy avoided giving Dominic advice. Instead she helped the teacher figure out workable solutions to his problem. She gave the teacher ownership of and responsibility for his issue or *monkey*. At the same time, through both her words and actions, the principal demonstrated her confidence in and support for the teacher. Cindy was a powerful speaker who chose her words with intention, avoided advice, used positive presuppositions, and asked Dominic powerful, open-ended questions. As a result of her changed approach to decision making in her school, Cindy also found more time to spend in classrooms—her original goal!

Ask Powerful Questions

One additional component of speaking powerfully during coaching conversations is learning to ask powerful questions. Our colleague, Sandee Crowther (2009), describes powerful questions as those that:

- Assume positive intent and focus on positive connections
- Are open-ended
- Invite multiple answers, not one correct answer
- Act as thought starters to energize the mind and consider new perspectives
- Focus on solutions, not problems
- Empower to help the other client go to a deeper level and uncover patterns of thinking.

Sample open-ended, powerful questions include:

- What strategies are you considering?
- What will your criteria include when you implement your plan?
- What barriers do you anticipate?
- What resources will help you?
- What additional information would help you make a decision about . . .?
- What successful approaches have you employed in similar situations that you could utilize now?

A school leader who assumes positive intent about his staff believes all staff members have the answers to their own issues and questions within them and that his role is to help others think deeply and make their own connections. By asking open-ended questions the leader fosters reflection and builds trust and relationships. Through powerful questions, the leader demonstrates that he values multiple solutions and answers. He is open to the thoughts of others, fosters their reflection, and demonstrates confidence in their abilities.

By focusing conversations on solution thinking rather than on problems, a school leader helps teachers recognize the power of positivity. Focusing on solutions leads us to imagine a bright future through action. Focusing on problems weighs us down in the past, wallowing in inaction.

Finally, powerful questions are empowering because they encourage people to dig deeper into their thinking, where they can discover those patterns that have led to accomplishments in the past and which may be applied in the current moment to generate success.

Questions that begin with *what* may be very powerful. For example, asking one of your teachers, "What has worked well for you in the past when dealing with a similar situation?" may cause that teacher to dig deeper into his thinking, form a positive connection between a successful event in the past and the present, and help him generate some ideas for action. At the same time, the teacher has an opportunity to become more confident in his abilities and you have demonstrated your trust in him, resulting in a stronger working relationship.

If this same teacher has difficulty with formulating his next steps, you might ask another powerful question, such as "What is the first important step that you want to take?" or "What are the two main points you want to include in your talk with the challenging student we have been discussing?" Additional examples of powerful questions are listed in Appendix A.

Summary

Conversations require both a speaker and a listener. Powerful speaking is integral when holding coaching conversations and is the flip side of committed listening. In this chapter, you learned the value of creating your intention for a coaching conversation. What is your goal or focus for speaking and how do you want to *be* in the conversation? Will you be open to alternative ideas? Are there some items that are non-negotiable? Coaching conversations require reflection before speaking.

After determining the intention for the coaching conversation, you explored the importance of choosing language that aligns your spoken words with your internal intention. School leaders tend to overuse both obligatory language and words of commitment. By choosing language that conveys precisely what you intend, your communication becomes clear and others learn that they can trust what you say to them.

By forming positive presuppositions that express positive intent, your coaching conversations communicate the belief that other people are capable and want to perform well. You do so by asking open-ended questions and making statements that convey your confidence in the other individual.

Powerful speakers avoid giving advice since solving problems for others sends the message that only they have the right answers and they want people to be dependent on them. Conversely, supporting others by encouraging them to think deeply and helping them generate their own solutions, conveys that you trust them and they are competent. By avoiding advice, you also save time because you are no longer taking on the responsibilities of other members of your school community. At the same time, staff members gain confidence in themselves and their level of trust with you increases.

Finally, you discovered that powerful questions provide opportunities for deep thinking and dialogue. Powerful questions focus on solutions for the future rather than problems from the past. They assume positive intent that each individual has the capability within him or herself to seek solutions. Your role in the coaching conversation is to help others think and make connections through the open-ended questions you ask.

5

Reflective Feedback

Feedback is a key contributor to motivation. The need to be valued is a potent emotional force, and positive feedback fills that need.

—David Sousa, "Brain-Friendly Learning for Teachers"

Especially in education, we are always being asked to give people feedback. Teachers give students feedback about their class work. Principals give teachers feedback about their instruction and achievement results. Superintendents give principals feedback about the success results in their schools. Many of these feedback comments could be categorized as judgment statements:

- "I like the way you . . ."
- "You are doing a good job at . . ."
- "I would like you to consider . . ."
- "Have you thought about . . .?"
- "Here is an area of concern . . ."

In this chapter you will learn

- The importance of feedback
- Three types of feedback
- Options to offer meaningful feedback
- How to Coach-on-the-Fly using reflective feedback
- How to structure a conversation about a difficult topic

> By learning to give good feedback, you become true partners with your colleagues.

By learning to give good feedback, you become true partners with your colleagues and build their capacity to be the best educators they can be.

The Importance of Feedback

David Sousa (2009), a consultant in educational neuroscience, suggests that feedback actually fuels learning. In his article "Brain-Friendly Learning for Teachers," Sousa discusses how areas of the brain are more active in subjects who are learning tasks and receiving feedback than in those subjects not receiving feedback. The feedback encouraged the learners and contributed to their motivation. Positive feedback filled the strong emotional need to be valued.

Constructive feedback acts in the same way. When it is timely, specific, and builds on others' strengths, it is very effective. But feedback is often neglected or given half-heartedly.

David Perkins (2003), author of *King Arthur's Round Table: How Collaborative Conversations Create Smart Organizations*, says there is good news and bad news about feedback. "The good news is that feedback is essential for individual, community, and organizational effectiveness and learning. The bad news is that feedback often flops, yielding no meaningful exchange of information and driving people apart" (p. 42). He offers some food for thinking about feedback and the possibilities of new responses for long-standing habits. He suggests there are two components to feedback. One is the content of the feedback— the message or information that you want to share. The other component is the importance and value of the relationship.

Perkins describes three types of feedback in common practice as people try to balance the message with the relationship.

Figure 5.1   Three Types of Feedback

The Good News: Feedback is essential for individual, community, and organizational effectiveness and learning.

The Bad News: Feedback often flops, yielding no meaningful exchange of information and driving people apart.

Negative Feedback

- The lay-it-on-the-line critical feedback
- The most painful type because it tells people straight out what's wrong
- It is most obvious to give and usually follows a natural avalanche of impulse, such as "That was awful," "Did you think?"
- People need to know what's wrong—so why not tell them: "too long," "boring," "uninteresting"
- The information can be alienating and over time can provoke defensiveness and negative attitudes
- Negative feedback is worsened when it focuses on a person's core identity rather than a product or an idea, that is, "It sounded stupid to me," "Last-minute Lucy, again."

Conciliatory Feedback

- Positive and vague. Avoids criticizing to be supportive and avoid conflict; comes from belief that negative feedback will be rejected and relationship harmed, such as "OK, that will probably work," "Interesting"
- Often called "social stroking"
- Usually read as pleasant, encouraging, and nonthreatening. Not feedback at all: it's encouragement and conflict avoidance in the guise of feedback
- Rationale: relationships are so important and feedback is so difficult—chooses relationships over information
- Receiver learns over multiple occasions that the feedback is empty and can be read as evasive or pandering

Communicative Feedback

- Clarifies an idea or behavior under consideration (to be sure you are talking about the same thing)
- Communicates positive features toward preserving and building upon them
- Communicates concerns and suggestions toward improvement
- Consumes more time, requires thought and effort
- Read as careful, respectful, and honest

Adapted from David Perkins (2003) *King Arthur's Round Table: How Collaborative Conversations Create Smart Organizations*

Three Types of Feedback

Figure 5.1 describes three types of feedback. The first type is *negative feedback*. This is the type people often use when they have suggestions to recommend for improvement. It is given (and received) as critical feedback. It is a lay-it-on-the-line message with no sugar coating. It can be very painful because it tells people very directly what is wrong. Negative feedback is at its worst when it is sarcastic or follows judgments about a person's core self—"Here comes Last Minute Lucy again!" or "That was stupid!"

One may ask, "Why not just tell people straight out what is wrong? It takes too long to 'dance' around the issues." However, information given in this way can be alienating. It most often provokes defensiveness and negative attitudes. The receivers of negative feedback go into protective mode and stop listening. They begin defending themselves almost immediately. Instead of listening to the desired changes, they formulate rebuttals and spend their time justifying what they are currently doing. The message is delivered but the feedback falls on deaf ears.

A second type of feedback is called *conciliatory feedback*. This kind of feedback is positive but vague. It avoids conflict and criticizing in order to appear supportive. It comes from the belief that negative feedback will be rejected and the relationship with the other person will be harmed. Examples include, "Interesting" or "That will probably work." Conciliatory feedback is read by receivers as pleasant, encouraging, and nonthreatening. But it is not feedback at all. As Perkins says, "It is encouragement and conflict avoidance in the guise of feedback" (2003, p. 44). The speaker is choosing relationship over message in the belief that maintaining the relationship is more important than delivering the message. Over time receivers may learn that the feedback is empty and could begin to read the feedback as superficial or evasive.

The third type of feedback is *communicative feedback*. In Perkins' words this type of feedback "clarifies the idea or behavior under consideration, communicates positive features worth preserving and builds upon them, and poses concerns and/or suggestions toward improvement" (2003, p. 46). It may take more time than the other two forms of feedback and certainly requires more thought and effort. However, Perkins notes that it is read by others as honest and respectful.

In the past people have talked about "warm" and "cool" feedback. *Warm* feedback was saying something positive about the topic. This was followed by *cool* feedback, which was saying something critical or more distanced. This type of feedback offered language for sharing information. Yet receivers were often confused about the *but* statement following the positive ones. They either did not clearly hear the *but* as something to take seriously or they focused too much on it to the exclusion of the strengths listed before it.

Options for Offering Meaningful Feedback

David Perkins (2003) suggests a new frame for offering meaningful feedback. He calls it *communicative feedback*. Instead of using warm and cool feedback, he suggests we offer feedback through the lens of three steps:

1. Clarifying questions or statements

2. Value statements or questions

3. Questions or possibility statements

Let's look at the feedback document in Figure 5.2.

Figure 5.2   Steps to Communicative Feedback

1. Ask clarifying questions for understanding:
   "How do you see this different from . . .?"
   "How did your students respond to the process?"
   "What are the costs you have calculated to put this in place?"
   "Of your resources you used, which ones would provide the most help to move forward?"

(Continued)

(Continued)

"Which groups provided useful input to the plan?"

"When you checked alignment with the state tests, what did you find as strengths or gaps?"

"What are you thinking will be a barrier for parents?"

2. Express the *value* potential specifically:

"The strength of the idea is . . ."

"You have really thought deeply about . . ."

"I see evidence of . . ."

"As a parent and teacher, the idea is very exciting to me because . . ."

"It provides high engagement for students by . . ."

"This could offer value to students by . . ."

"The scaffolding of your design will help others understand . . ."

3. Offer reflective questions or possibilities:

"What are you considering in regard to . . .?"

"I wonder what would happen if . . ."

"I'm wondering if you noticed any gaps in student understanding."

"What other considerations are you thinking about?"

"To align more closely with the state tests, what if . . .?"

"What connections have you made to . . . (other subjects, real world, state testing)?"

Adapted from David Perkins (2003) *King Arthur's Round Table: How Collaborative Conversations Create Smart Organizations*

Clarifying questions and statements are often used as the first step in giving communicative feedback to others. They get a conversation started.

- They ask for more information from the other person. "How did your students respond to the process?"
- They are often rooted in concepts or ideas about which the speaker is curious. "Which groups provided useful input into the plan?"
- They seek to make underlying assumptions explicit. "How do you see this different from . . .?"

Clarifying statements are also very useful for naming or labeling the topic under discussion. They make the core subject explicit and create an "anticipatory set" for the conversation. For example, "I would like to discuss differentiated instruction in your lesson today." We will talk more about this later in the chapter.

Value statements express the value potential of the person or the topic of discussion.

- They affirm a specific strength observed in the other person. "You have really thought about this deeply."
- They identify the positive actions that are observed in the situation. "I see evidence of . . ."
- They make explicit the speaker's bias toward the topic. "It provides high engagement for students by . . ."

Reflective questions or possibilities engage the thinking of the other person and request a response.

- They take the spotlight off the speaker and shine it on the other person. "What are you considering in regard to . . .?"
- They push the thinking of the other person to make new connections and see other points of view. "What connections have you made to . . . (other subjects, real world, state testing)?"
- They ask for creative or out-of-the-box thinking. "I wonder what would happen if . . .?"

This kind of feedback is specific and builds on people's strengths. It assumes positive intent (There is that *forming positive presuppositions* when speaking powerfully again!). It changes the conversation from the speaker doing all the talking and thinking to a true dialogue between two people. For this reason we call it *reflective feedback* because it reduces potential for defensiveness and engages the other person in deep reflection and possibility thinking. When done well the person giving feedback speaks less than the person to whom the conversation is addressed. The purpose is to bring forward the thinking of the teacher, to help him better understand his own practices, and become able to intentionally use new practices more strategically.

Examples of reflective feedback might be

- What are your criteria for being a *successful student* in your class?
- What are indicators that your students are good at critical thinking?
- What were the key factors that made this project successful for students?
- How can you apply something you have done successfully in the past to this situation?
- *Why* do you like it? What specifically makes it work well?
- Additional examples of reflective feedback are in Appendix B.

Coaching-on-the-Fly

Principals and other leaders can also use these reflective feedback stems individually as frames for responding to interactions during the course of their busy days. We call it Coaching-on-the-Fly. What principal hasn't had a teacher stop her in the hall and tell her some wonderful story about a just-finished class lesson? The principal doesn't have time for a full conversation, but she could respond using one of these frames. It might sound like this:

- "I can tell you are very excited about the learning that lesson generated!" (*value potential*)

      or

- "What did students learn better with this activity than they had with the previous way you taught it?" (*clarifying question*)

      or

- "What are ways to apply what you have just learned to other content?" (*possibility thinking*)

Responding to something a person tells you in this way demonstrates thought and concern. It offers something to consider further (personal observation, inference, data, or reflective question) rather than simply giving a judgment—either positive or negative, such as "Good job!" or "Wonderful!"

Feedback Practice

Practice giving feedback and Coaching-on-the-Fly by responding to any of these situations that a colleague may bring to you:

- A problem of low-performing students
- Instruction that did or did not get results
- Strategies for issues of discipline
- Ways to work with difficult students or parents
- Reflections about a past performance at a faculty meeting, professional development session, or parent meeting

Which of the response steps do you use most easily—clarifying questions, value potential, or reflective questions? This knowledge will help you focus your thinking when a colleague asks your opinion. You learn to think about what kind of question to ask *rather than* how the problem might be solved. Because you want colleagues to come to their own solutions, you focus your energy on framing *good questions* to ask.

> Because you want colleagues to come to their own solutions, you focus your energy on framing good questions to ask.

Framing an Important Conversation Using Reflective Feedback

These reflective feedback steps may also be used together to form a *frame* for starting an important or difficult conversation that you might want to have. The process is shown in Figure 5.3.

Figure 5.3   Difficult Conversation Frame

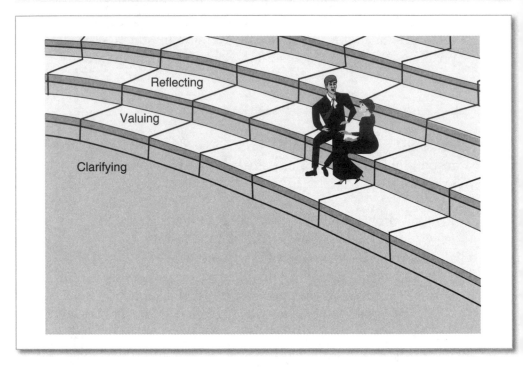

Say for instance that you have a good "meat and potatoes" teacher. She is dedicated, resourceful, and straight forward. You have observed in her classroom and would like her to use more teaching strategies that differentiate instruction to better meet the needs of the gifted students in her class. Using reflective feedback as a *conversation frame*, you would put the three steps together.

1. The first step is to *clarify* or *name* what you want to discuss. In this case you are using a clarifying statement.

Example: "Mrs. Barker, today I'd like to talk about differentiated instruction."

There is no guessing or hedging about what the topic is.

2. The second step is to *identify the value* that you hold for the topic or the value that you see in the other person or both.

Example: "You are a teacher who really wants each of your students to reach their potential and I believe that differentiated instruction is a good tool for that purpose." Here you acknowledge her commitment to her students and the value you see in differentiated instruction.

3. The third step is to ask a question that opens *possibility thinking*.

Example: "What are the ways you typically plan for differentiated instruction in your lessons?" This uses a positive presupposition that opens up the conversation for her to respond without being defensive.

What you say to frame the conversation should not take more than one minute. This leaves the majority of the talk time with the teacher. When done well the person giving feedback speaks less than the person to whom the conversation is addressed. Consider the following example:

Principal Terry has a concern about Caroline, a conscientious technology teacher who has been giving many failing grades to students on their projects. He suspects she has been using grades as a discipline hammer instead of as a tool to assess and give feedback to students about their actual work products. Principal Terry has regular monthly meetings with each of his teachers and during one with Caroline he began the conversation like this. "Caroline, today I would like to talk about what goes into assigning grades in your class (clarifying the topic of discussion). I know that you want students to take your class seriously and create substantive products in their projects (value potential). How do you communicate your high standards to your students? (reflective question)".

Over the next 10 minutes, Caroline talked about the criteria she used to grade student projects. She said she was frustrated this year because the students seemed more immature than in previous years. They spent a lot of time goofing off in class and not using class time wisely. They appeared to just throw something together at the last minute to submit for their projects. Many students clearly were not demonstrating the knowledge and skills she expected in her class. Terry asked if there were another way to structure the grading so it did not all happen at the end of a project. Caroline remembered that she had done some projects in the past, especially ones with long timelines in stages. She had established criteria to meet for each stage. Maybe she could work out something like that for even the shorter projects. But then she remembered why she stopped doing it that way: That meant there was a lot more grading on her part.

So Terry asked her if there were other ways she might consider to give students feedback about their projects without it all coming from her. Caroline thought a minute and then said this might be a place for peer reviews. Or maybe she could walk around the room as students worked and do informal "grading" and feedback during class time.

Then Terry asked, "What will be your evidence that this new way of grading in stages is working?" Caroline quickly said, "I'll know it is working if the projects I receive at the end are better quality than what I currently get. All of these students are capable of getting As and Bs in this class. But instead, many are getting Ds and Fs right now. If I set criteria for each stage of the project and give informal feedback to students along the way, it is worth the extra work to have them really learn what I want them to learn."

Caroline left the principal's office with a plan she had designed herself and Principal Terry made a commitment to Caroline to support her in these efforts to find alternative ways to engage and involve students in creating quality work.

Note that in this example Terry did not tell Caroline what to do. He simply set the stage for her to "think out loud" about how she might change her instruction and feedback to possibly get better results with students. He believed she was a capable teacher and gave her support and encouragement to try some new ideas to reach a challenging group of students.

Journal Reflection About an Important Upcoming Conversation

Using a journal, explore the reflective feedback steps to frame an important or difficult conversation you want to have with someone.

- What will be the clarifying step? Will it be a question or a statement?
- What value do you want to identify in the other person or in the topic idea?
- What questions might open possibility thinking or reflection for the other person?

With whom might you practice saying these three steps in less than one minute before you have your "important conversation?" How is this process of reflective feedback different from the usual way you respond? What is the potential of this language of reflective feedback to change and improve communication among staff?

Using the Reflective Feedback Frame to Support Excellence

Note that the format for reflective feedback is also an excellent frame to use for evaluation conferences. It can be used to deliver good feedback as well as "improvement needed" feedback. It uses "coach-like" language to structure the conversation. It stretches teachers' thinking while also acknowledging their individual strengths. It is a very powerful way to frame these conversations—especially with excellent teachers—and generates feelings of confidence and competence on the part of great teachers.

> The format for reflective feedback is an excellent frame to use for evaluation conferences.

Hilda was an outstanding kindergarten teacher. In her school, in which 75% of the families qualified for free or reduced-price meals, she nurtured young children's curiosity, disciplined with steadiness and warmth, developed academic skills using meaningful connections, and partnered with families to create a positive experience for children's first contact with school. In addition, Hilda was respected by colleagues, a vocal advocate for child-centered education on district committees, and considered a "star" teacher by her principal.

In the past when Principal David had met with Hilda for her evaluation conference, he had recited in glowing details all the things that he had observed about Hilda's teaching and her role as an educational leader—both at the school and for the district. After 15 minutes of reporting Hilda's great qualities as a teacher, the formal document was signed by both and then the rest of the half hour was used for informal chit-chat about school or personal things.

This year David wanted a more substantive exchange to occur during the evaluation conference. He decided to put some of his new coach-like skills to work. He said, "Hilda, over the past year I have been especially interested in your work with children who come with very little school background (clarifying statement). You are able to ignite their energy and learning potential to acquire basic literacy and numeracy skills (value potential). What are ways you find to be particularly helpful in creating that teaching 'magic'?" (reflective question). Then he was quiet and for the next 29 minutes, Hilda and he engaged in deep conversation about her educational philosophy, her beliefs about how young children learn, and her reflections about what works in the classroom.

When the conference time was over, Hilda thanked the principal for listening and helping her articulate in her own mind what the reasons were for her success in the classroom. These factors were certainly ideas that would help her in working as a mentor with novice teachers—something she would really love to do someday. Principal David had not assigned Hilda mentor duties in the past for fear of overloading her with outside responsibilities. After this conversation he assured Hilda that she would definitely be assigned a novice to mentor the following school year.

Hilda danced out the principal's door, feeling very competent and confident—not from the observations of her principal, but from the brilliance he had allowed to emerge from her speaking about her practices. The principal gained not only a great mentor from this conversation but also great esteem and appreciation from Hilda about his leadership ability!

Summary

In this chapter you have learned how important giving meaningful feedback is to the learning of others. When you are honest and straightforward with others about addressing important issues and concerns, you earn a reputation of being courageous and skillful in communicating.

You also explored three kinds of feedback and learned some steps for giving feedback in a new, more powerful way. It is important to remember that the gift of good reflective feedback goes both ways. If we model giving good feedback to others, we have to be willing to hear feedback from others about ourselves. While it may be difficult to hear others' truths about ourselves, there is likely to be a vein of gold worth mining.

Finally, you have looked at how to use the reflective feedback structure as a way to frame important or difficult conversations. By speaking your truth honestly and listening to the truths others share about your behavior, conversations become more authentic and your relationships with people become deeper and more profound. You truly can learn to say what you mean without being mean!

6

Putting It All Together

A Way of Being

*King Author's dream was people coming together to coor-
dinate their thoughts and efforts smoothly, effectively,
intelligently . . . just as neurons connect one part of the
brain to another, conversations connect the different parts
of communities and organizations. Conversations are the
virtual neurons of a collective mind.*

—David Perkins, *King Arthur's Round Table*

In the preceding five chapters we have proposed that leaders can use coach-like conversations as a significant tool to
transform their schools. We have described key skills to learning how to initiate these coach-like conversations, including:

- Being a committed listener
- Speaking with intention
- Focusing on the positive

- Avoiding advice
- Asking powerful questions
- Offering reflective feedback

In this chapter we will put the skills together and share two case studies in which significant changes occurred in schools because of the coaching conversations that occurred with and by the school leader. These examples are actual situations from our coaching practice. The names have been changed to protect the confidentiality of our clients.

The first case study demonstrates the transformative power of coaching within a single conversation while the second case study demonstrates how coaching conversations over time change how people think and act.

Case Study 1: Linda's Coaching Conversation

In this first case study from Linda Gross Cheliotes' experience, major coaching behaviors are identified in parentheses. Note that in a coaching conversation, the various coaching techniques weave throughout the interaction. They are not utilized in a sequential or isolated manner. Committed listening, especially by valuing silence and paying attention to the essence of what the other person says, is foundational to the process of holding a coaching conversation.

Background

Marcella is the lead science teacher in her large, urban kindergarten through eighth-grade school. She recognizes that among her strengths she is very knowledgeable, dependable, and conscientious about her job and personal responsibilities, responsive to the needs of others, and is a caring and kind person. Marcella enjoys working with most of the teachers in her school and she is proud that they genuinely appreciate her help.

One teacher, Jose, however, rarely teaches the required science curriculum and his past encounters with Marcella have been prickly and unproductive. The principal has now told Marcella that he expects her to turn the situation around and get Jose to implement the science curriculum, especially since the state testing program is just two months away.

Linda's Coaching Conversation

When Marcella brought this challenge to our coaching conversation, I asked her why she thought Jose was so resistant to teaching science *(clarifying question)*. Her immediate response was that Jose had had problems working with the math specialist, too. Sensing that Marcella was uncomfortable and self-protective *(committed listening)*, I asked her to reflect on the many reasons someone might resist teaching a required subject and curriculum *(powerful questioning)*. At this point Marcella was able to move away from becoming defensive and enumerate a variety of possibilities *(silence resulting in reflection):*

1. The teacher might not understand the curriculum

2. He might need additional training

3. Materials could be missing

4. The teacher might lack confidence in teaching science

5. He could be having personal problems that took time and energy away from class preparation

6. The teacher might be embarrassed about asking for help

Once Marcella had delineated an extensive list of possibilities for Jose's "prickly" behavior, I noticed that her tone of voice had become softer and less strained and her breathing had slowed *(listening for the essence)*.

Now that Marcella was in a calmer, less emotional state, I sensed that she was ready to dig a bit deeper and reflect on the situation with Jose on a different level *(committed listening leading to reflection)*. From prior conversations, I knew that Marcella had very capably handled other difficult situations and people, and I wondered what was different about her interactions with Jose. I decided to ask her about this by starting with a positive presupposition, "Marcella, you are a friendly and effective lead teacher, and you go out of your way to be open to your colleagues and help them feel comfortable working with you. I am wondering what is different in your interactions with Jose" *(value potential and reflective feedback)*.

After about 30 seconds of silent reflection, Marcella excitedly responded, "I just had an aha moment. I just realized that I have the same kind of interactions and reactions with my older brother! He never wants advice or help from me, even when he knows I am capable. We end up just glaring at each other. I just want my brother to acknowledge and respect me for what I bring to the situation. I guess I want the same from Jose" *(silence leading to deep insight)*.

We discussed Marcella's feelings and reactions for a few more minutes until she felt comfortable moving forward *(committed listening and clarifying statements)*. She still needed to work with Jose and it was now time to use her personal insights to move to action. She recognized that she could not force him to change but she could change her approach to Jose with the goal of providing a safe space for him to respond at least neutrally, if not positively to her offers of help in teaching science. I asked Marcella what she could do to adjust her own reactions to Jose *(open-ended question, generating possibilities)*. Marcella decided on several steps:

1. Monitor her breathing and intentionally focus her awareness on her mental and emotional reactions as she prepared for the meeting with Jose

2. Develop several positive presupposition stems about Jose, such as "As a teacher dedicated to your students' academic success . . ."

3. Prepare a series of safe open-ended questions she could ask him about teaching science, for example, "What two areas of the science curriculum do you think include the most engaging activities for students and what areas do you think need revision?" (*Notice the embedded positive presupposition that Jose is familiar with the curriculum and monitors his students' reactions to lessons*)

4. Schedule the meeting with Jose within the next three days

5. Offer Jose several meeting times in writing rather than interrupt his class to set up an appointment

6. Interact calmly with Jose and treat him respectfully

7. Bring the conversation to a close if she felt herself becoming annoyed or angry with Jose

8. Acknowledge that her negative responses to Jose were rooted in a long personal history

By the end of our coaching conversation, Marcella felt calm and confident and was actually looking forward to meeting with Jose. She knew that she could face this challenging encounter by utilizing coach-like behaviors of committed listening, starting the conversation by stating a positive presupposition, reflection, generating possibilities, focusing on asking powerful, open-ended questions, and avoiding giving Jose advice.

Case Study 2: Marceta's Series of Coaching Conversations

In this second case study from author Marceta Fleming Reilly's experience, you are encouraged to identify the coaching strategies used in this series of coaching conversations. What does the coach say and do and what impact do her coaching behaviors have on the client?

Background

Pat came to coaching as a referral from her superintendent. The superintendent told Marceta that Pat was an experienced principal but new to the district. She had a difficult staff and was trying to implement some big changes in the school that the board and superintendent supported. She thought Pat might benefit from having a coach.

Coaching Conversations Over Time

Pat and I established rapport very quickly, so I began probing to find out as much information as possible about Pat's perceived strengths and her core values. Through our conversations and the use of a "core values checklist" tool, Pat easily identified her strengths: organized, persistent, problem solver, knowledgeable about curriculum, loves data, cares about people, develops relationships over time, reflective.

Then I had her complete the sentence, "Things don't go well when. . . ." Here were some of her responses:

- Decisions aren't made and issues drag on
- People are slow to "get it" (She called this "slug" behavior)
- People expect me to be a "cheerleader" or to "schmooze"
- Relationships are phony
- Passive-aggressive behavior persists
- People play power/control games
- People play politics

From this list I could see that she was concerned about resistance among her staff members to the new ideas she wanted to bring to the school and frustrated with "games." I asked Pat, "Tell me what your vision is for your school culture." She talked about wanting her staff members to be "true collaborators" and for them to have a "strong commitment to good instruction." At the end of the session, I asked her to write a two-sentence vision statement as her work before our next call. "What do you want the adults to be doing in your school?"

During our next call we refined her vision to three clear statements about what she wanted in her school:

1. "I want staff to support and collaborate with each other."

2. "I want student learning to be the focus of instruction."

3. "I want staff to create common learning goals, assessments, and performance criteria within and across grade levels."

Then we discussed how she wanted to communicate this vision to her staff at a leadership team meeting she was having that afternoon.

Pat was very excited on her next call. The leadership team meeting had gone very well. Many of the concepts in her vision were embraced by the team members. As a group, they spontaneously generated ideas to support her vision when she asked them to create two lists:

1. What would students be doing in the *ideal* classroom?

2. What would teachers be doing in the *ideal* classroom?

Next she had the leadership team identify which items on these lists were consistently occurring now in classrooms and which items were occurring some of the time. As a follow-up she planned to have them rank which items were extremely necessary for an *ideal* classroom and which were nice but not essential.

During our coaching she reflected about what ideas generated by the teachers paralleled her vision and what meeting processes worked. Then I asked her, "What do you want as norms for your future teacher meetings?" She generated four norms that she believed were important for her future meetings:

1. Meetings are a safe environment for brainstorming and sharing ideas

2. Willingness to share ideas

3. All ideas presented are respected

4. Risk taking is encouraged (proposing new, far-out, alternative or fringe ideas)

Coach's Meta-Thinking

At the beginning Pat was very frustrated because a few staff members were continuously arguing about her decisions and pushing back about the boundaries. I did not know what the problem was, but I knew that it was important for her to be clear about what she wanted (her vision) and to acknowledge the values and strengths she had to draw upon. I asked her questions about her vision: "What would it look like? Sound like?" I also asked her, "With whom is it most important to share your vision?" These questions helped her think about ways to share her clear vision with others.

By using this self-knowledge with her leadership team, she found that many of her key teachers wholeheartedly agreed with her ideas. This gave her confidence and courage to continue to move forward with vision sharing.

Pat took this experience and began to apply it to an upcoming parent orientation meeting. She wanted to develop parent support for the changes she wanted to make in the school. She identified some stories of students to highlight and explain her vision to parents in a clear, graphic way. Her messages to the parents included:

- This school is a warm and nurturing place
- We value student-focused instruction and learning
- Students have individual needs
- We want parents to be involved and give us input

In her response form after our coaching session Pat said discussing the parent orientation in this way really helped her focus on key points. She was able to personalize the presentation more and let herself shine through. She was more relaxed and knew she ultimately wanted to convey that she cares about kids and families and wants each child to be successful. She focused on building connections and giving honest answers. The parents seemed to appreciate this.

In our fourth call Pat described her stress with teachers who were constantly pushing the boundaries she set and arguing with her about rules. So we discussed her decision-making parameters. I asked her, "How do you make your non-negotiables clear?" She told me she tried to listen with an open ear and admitted that she sometimes agreed to the teacher request just to get them out of the office. She wanted to be open to teacher ideas, but she had been compromising her standards. As a result, things which were not aligned with her vision were happening in the school. Pat acknowledged that this situation had developed because of her efforts to "be nice" to teachers.

I asked what she wanted instead. Pat was clear that she wanted to work with staff in collaborative ways, but she was learning that she wanted to be more honest with the staff. She wanted to let them know clearly the alternatives with which she could happily live and those issues on which she could not compromise. She wanted to set clear limits and expectations about how decisions would be made in the future and explain how she and staff could work together in decision making.

Here is what she wrote after this call:

> "I have become more aware that in my desire to accommodate my teachers or seem open to their ideas, I send mixed messages. While I thought I was accepting options that I could live with, I realized that I was really compromising my beliefs in order to make teachers happy. Most of all I wasn't doing what was best for kids. I have become much more aware of how I respond to the teachers and what I say and do."

Coach's Meta-Thinking

By talking about the criteria she uses to make decisions and then having her apply that criteria to her recent interactions with teachers, Pat realized that she was contributing to the overall confusion of staff by "giving in" on things that were not aligned with her vision and values. In other ways I also practiced pushing Pat's thinking. I frequently asked, "What did you learn? What are you teaching yourself? What made that work or not work?" This helped her reflect about her behavior and the consequent actions more deeply.

Over the next few months Pat really put her learning into practice and I saw much growth in her leadership development. We discussed many situations in her through the lens of these questions:

- What did she want?
- What was the framework within which she could compromise?
- Whose decision was it?

She learned that the clearer she could be in stating what she wanted, the quicker the staff learned they could not negotiate to get back their old way. Pat's superintendent gave her appreciative comments about how much progress the Building Leadership team was making and Pat noted that staff seemed more open and relaxed.

Over time, I began to see a negative pattern developing when she planned for work with the fifth-grade team. This was the group of teachers who had been most resistant to her leadership during the past year. Her thinking would start with predicting how badly the fifth-grade teachers would respond and then move to figuring out ways to confront and respond authentically.

I noted this pattern and asked her if any of the fifth-grade teachers had strengths that would fit into her vision for the school. She was able to list strengths for each teacher. So then we discussed how she might build upon these strengths rather than working from their conflicts. This was difficult for her. She was so used to seeing them as adversaries that it was hard to see through to the positive. We talked about ways she had worked with children and other groups of teachers to support and build on strengths rather then working from deficits.

Over the next two calls she became very clear about what she wanted from this team:

- Talk about student work and exchange sound teaching ideas
- Teach units together
- Share their strengths by
  - Talking about instructional philosophies
  - Learning from each other

Coach's Meta-Thinking

When I asked Pat to consider the strengths of each of the fifth-grade teachers, I was offering a different point of view for her to consider the situation. This was a new vantage point for her and difficult because she had been seeing them as adversaries rather than allies. Once she shifted to thinking of them as allies for teaching children, her attitude and her "edge" softened. She was able to approach the group differently (more respectfully) and they responded to her differently. She got different results than she had in the past.

Pat decided she wanted to do some team-building/trust-building activities with her whole staff. She felt that everyone could benefit from such work together. She continued to set clear expectations about what she wanted and to create the new, collaborative culture for her school. The district was also supporting the direction she was going with her school and she saw that she and her school could be a leader in the changes the superintendent wanted to make in the district. My role during this period was to help Pat find ways to clearly express her expectations while listening to the needs of others. I would ask questions such as:

- "What are your goals for this meeting or activity?"
- "What are your expectations for the group?"
- "How will you model collaboration?"

- "How will this meeting or activity contribute to your vision and help build trust among the participants?"
- "What might be a win-win solution that does not compromise your basic beliefs?"

Through this work Pat began to focus on leading with her strengths, which were knowledge of curriculum and experience in facilitating professional learning. She became less concerned about beating back "adversaries" and more focused on creating a school team.

In July our conversations turned to planning for the upcoming year. One third of her teachers would be new due to a shift in attendance patterns in the district. Elementary schools were combining and her school would become the Grades 3–5 unit and her "sister" school would house the kindergarten through second-grade students.

She worked with the combined Building Leadership team during the late spring and summer. She was excited about the new teachers who were joining her staff because she felt they had strong instructional skills and were coming from a school that had a very collaborative environment. She felt they would be good role models for the kind of culture she wanted in her school.

Here were some goals Pat set for her new school:

- There would be a collaborative environment among teachers and all staff.
- Core beliefs existed among staff with which Pat agreed. Her role would be to help make these beliefs consistent and pervasive throughout the school.
- Expectations for the children would flow from the beliefs and vision they shared. This would be the standard for decision making.
- Staff meetings would be spent on celebrating successes and helping each other with problems (modeling collaboration).

Pat's new desire was to balance setting clear expectations without being a dictator. Her work with her Building

Leadership team during the summer was paying off. There was high morale and positive interaction with her and among the members. They were responding well to her leadership—recognizing her strengths in curriculum and instruction and moving forward without complaint. She found that setting clear expectations and being explicit with her vision was very helpful to the staff. Even the "difficult" teachers from the previous year were less argumentative and more receptive to the changes.

In August we began looking at the "bigger picture" for her school. What did she want to communicate to her teachers by her very presence?

- What is best for kids is my priority in decision making.
- I know there is great instruction going on in every classroom.
- We can learn from each other and solve problems better if we work together.
- I have knowledge in curriculum and instruction and want to help in these areas.
- I believe in looking at data before taking action.
- I am honest and persistent in my ways.

With these ideas in mind, how would she set the faculty meeting norms? Work with the Building Leadership team? Structure her communications and interactions with district office personnel and parents? Work with teachers who were ignoring requested changes?

Pat thought about ways to communicate appreciation of her teachers' strengths and model collaboration using core beliefs as the lens for making decisions. She later celebrated that the transition was going very smoothly. The building norms had emerged very nicely and had already been used to resolve a problem. Her most difficult fifth-grade teacher was following the rules, no longer arguing with her or subverting her desires. And she was communicating more openly and honestly with district office personnel, delivering her message without blame or emotional load.

Coach's Meta-Thinking

I really began to push Pat to consider the "bigger game." We were doing a lot of problem solving as she planned for the new school year with her new staff. I wanted to take problem solving to the next level—beyond the immediate concern. What was the "big idea"? How do you want to be in a situation? This was very fruitful. It enabled her to see issues in broader contexts and to make connections from one situation to another. This is when she devised her meeting norms and considered what be-ing she wanted to communicate from the very first day of school with staff, students, and parents.

In our final call Pat said that coaching helped her clearly define what she wanted and articulate this to others. She said she found that she had many answers within herself, but before coaching, she did not have the confidence or courage to put them into practice. During coaching she worked to change two habits:

1. Trying to please everyone by taking ownership of others' problems to "fix" everything

2. Sending mixed messages

Through coaching she had learned to distinguish between a problem that was hers and one that was not. And most importantly, she had also become clearer and more direct in her messages to others.

Coaching Goals and Insights

During the time I was coaching Pat, I became aware that I was mentoring some clients rather than coaching them— coaxing them to one or another solution that I thought best or outright giving advice about situations. Therefore I became very intentional about trying to separate my coaching from my mentoring. I tried to be transparent when I was mentoring, ask permission before I did it, and most importantly, to be intentional about *not* doing it.

I intentionally planned for and practiced using question stems that I hoped would take my client to deeper levels of thinking and give her a new perspective to consider. My goal became one of trying to make each conversation count—to help my client discover something new, and gain confidence and strength from each conversation.

I saw Pat grow from a person who was frustrated because a few staff members were continuously arguing about her decisions and not accepting her leadership to a person who clearly articulated her expectations and values while listening with care to the needs of others. She sought the win-win solution wherever she could as long as her basic beliefs were not compromised. I believe that coaching helped her find her "leadership voice."

Next Steps

Throughout *Coaching Conversations: Transforming Your School One Conversation at a Time* we have included examples of specific coaching skills, stems for questions and digging deeper into conversations, and ended by presenting samples of full coaching conversations with numerous coaching behaviors interwoven throughout the interactions.

We believe that leadership that includes skillful use of coach-like conversations creates a culture of capability and possibility in schools for the teachers who work there and the students who attend. Coaching skill is not easy to develop. It is, in fact, counterintuitive to the typical way we think about leadership happening. Instead of being the problem solver and idea generator, the leader becomes the keeper of the vision and the one who helps *others* succeed. Such leadership can only thrive in an environment with high relational trust. Coach-like leaders are credible and they walk their talk.

> Coach-like leaders are credible and they walk their talk.

As Dennis Sparks (2007) alluded in the foreword of this book, leaders must understand that coaching is not about manipulating people to do what you want them to do. It is about authentically listening, holding oneself accountable, and intentionally focusing efforts to develop the capacity of others. It is "servant leadership." To learn to do coach-like conversations well, one must practice over time and have a "critical friend" to give them honest feedback about their progress.

As a new practitioner of coaching conversations, we recommend that you first focus on one particular skill, such as listening to others without piggybacking on their stories (autobiographical listening) or asking open-ended questions. Consciously practice this skill until it becomes a habit of mind. For some, journaling observations about your application of coaching skills and the impact these behaviors have on other people fosters learning. For others, sharing your learning goals with a trusted friend or colleague will provide incentive for mastering new skills. See Figure 6.1 below.

Figure 6.1 Next Steps Checklist

In his review of brain research, David Rock (2006) found that forming "new habits takes time, but not that much" (p. 24). You should be able to develop specific coach-like behaviors through consistent and intentional practice of individual skills for one to two weeks each. Within a period of several months you will have a broad repertoire of skills that will permit you to hold meaningful and constructive coaching conversations. Below is a list of some new conversational habits you may wish to practice.

☐ Practice one committed listening skill with a trusted friend, family member, or colleague.

- Listen for the essence of what is said or not said
- Allow time for silence after someone speaks with you
- Avoid unproductive listening (judgment/criticism, piggybacking, inquisitive listening, problem solving)
- Listen without obligation to act
- Begin using your committed listening skills with your staff
- Paraphrase what others say to you

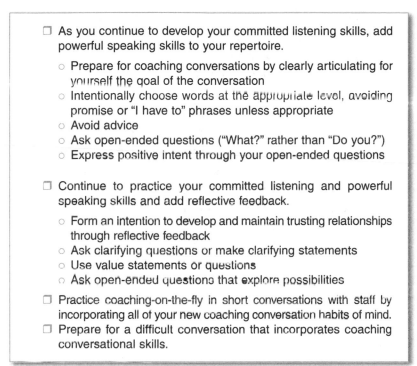

□ As you continue to develop your committed listening skills, add powerful speaking skills to your repertoire.
  ○ Prepare for coaching conversations by clearly articulating for yourself the goal of the conversation
  ○ Intentionally choose words at the appropriate level, avoiding promise or "I have to" phrases unless appropriate
  ○ Avoid advice
  ○ Ask open-ended questions ("What?" rather than "Do you?")
  ○ Express positive intent through your open-ended questions

□ Continue to practice your committed listening and powerful speaking skills and add reflective feedback.
  ○ Form an intention to develop and maintain trusting relationships through reflective feedback
  ○ Ask clarifying questions or make clarifying statements
  ○ Use value statements or questions
  ○ Ask open-ended questions that explore possibilities

□ Practice coaching-on-the-fly in short conversations with staff by incorporating all of your new coaching conversation habits of mind.
□ Prepare for a difficult conversation that incorporates coaching conversational skills.

As you become comfortable integrating one coaching skill into your daily conversations, challenge yourself by adding a new coaching skill to your repertoire. Over time you will notice that you are engaging in full coaching conversations. We encourage you to acknowledge and celebrate your growth and the positive impact you are having on your school community.

Finally, one of the most helpful strategies for learning how to transform your school through coaching conversations is to work with a skillful school leadership coach, who will support you as you develop and achieve your goals. Through such a relationship you will personally experience the transformative power of coaching.

Summary

Coaching is such a privilege. It allows leaders to work very closely with others to help them find their passions, rediscover their strengths, and build from there. In the process leaders learn ever more about themselves, about ways of being with others, and are challenged to *be* more themselves. In a good coaching relationship both client and coach learn and grow.

The individual coaching conversations in which you engage have the power to transform your school. Employing coach-like behaviors of committed listening, powerful speaking, and reflective feedback communicate strong messages to your staff, students, parents, colleagues, and community members, that you value and respect them. Moreover, you convey your belief in their personal brilliance to reflect, generate possibilities, plan, and execute solutions. Through coaching conversations you authentically demonstrate trust and collaboration—the hallmarks of 21st-century leadership.

Appendices

Appendix A

Powerful, Open-Ended Questions

Powerful, open-ended questions require more than a *yes* or *no* response. They stimulate thinking and reflection. Powerful questions lay the groundwork for moving forward with action and change.

Samples of Powerful Open-Ended Questions

- What new structures are you putting into place to achieve your instructional goal?
- Because the success of your students is your passion, what strategies are you considering . . . ?
- When you faced a similar dilemma, what course of action did you find most helpful?
- What is the most important outcome for our conversation?
- What similarities are there between this situation and . . . ?
- What are the benefits of . . . ?
- How would you like to be in your interactions with parents?
- Since collaboration with colleagues is a core value in our school, what plans are you considering for developing lessons with teachers in your department?
- What resources will you need to . . . ?
- What are you taking away from our conversation today?

- What is the most challenging part?
- On a scale of 1 to 10, how important is this to you?
- How do you feel about the amount of time you are putting into . . . ?
- How can I best help you think this through?
- What do you need to do to . . . ?
- What are the next steps?
- What have you learned from . . . ?

Appendix B

Reflective Feedback

Reflective feedback provides specific information to others while also maintaining trust within relationships. There are three types of reflective feedback:

1. Clarifying questions or statements

2. Value potential statements

3. Questions or possibility statements

Samples of Clarifying Questions or Statements

- What responses did you receive from . . . ?
- Which resources were the most useful?
- When you checked the curriculum for alignment with state tests, what did you discover?
- I would like to discuss student engagement in the lesson.
- The goal for this meeting is . . .
- Let's review what you have decided so far.

Samples of Value Potential Statements

- You have really thought deeply about . . .
- There is evidence of . . .

- The strength of the idea is . . .
- Your idea is very exciting because . . .

Samples of Questions or Possibility Statements

- What other considerations are you thinking about?
- What learning gaps, if any, have you noticed in your Title 1 students' understanding of . . . ?
- I wonder what would happen if . . . ?
- What goals have your teachers set for differentiating instruction?

References

Blanchard, B., Oncken Jr., W., & Burrows, H. (1989). *The one minute manager meets the monkey.* New York: Quill/William Morrow.

Burley-Allen, M. (1999). *Communication self-assessment evaluation.* Retrieved on December 17, 2009, from www.dynamics-hb.com

Coaching For Results, Inc. (2007). *Strategies for powerful leading.* Retrieved on December 20, 2009, from www.coachingschoolre sults.com

Crowther, S. (2009). A second look at powerful questions. Retrieved on February 19, 2010, from http://www.coachingschoolresults .com/newsletters/0509.htm

Ellis, D. (Ed.). (2000). *Falling awake.* Rapid City, SD: Breakthrough Enterprises.

Fullan, M. (2006). *Turnaround leadership.* San Francisco: Jossey-Bass.

Payne, C. (2008). *So much reform, so little change.* Cambridge, MA: Harvard Education Press.

Perkins, D. (2003). *King Arthur's round table: How collaborative conversations create smart organizations.* Hoboken, NJ: John Wiley & Sons.

Rock, D. (2006). *Quiet leadership.* New York: HarperCollins

Scott, S. (2004). *Fierce conversations.* New York: Berkley.

Sousa, D. (2009). Brain-friendly learning for teachers. *Educational Leadership, 66*(9), Retrieved August 24, 2009, from http://www .ascd.org/publications/educational_leadership/summer09/v01 66/num09/Brain-Friendly_Learning_for_Teachers.aspx

Sparks, D. (2007). *Leading for results* (2nd ed.). Thousand Oaks, CA: Corwin.

Index

Page references followed by (figure) indicate an illustrated figure.

CORWIN

A SAGE Company

The Corwin logo—a raven striding across an open book—represents the union of courage and learning. Corwin is committed to improving education for all learners by publishing books and other professional development resources for those serving the field of PreK–12 education. By providing practical, hands-on materials, Corwin continues to carry out the promise of its motto: **"Helping Educators Do Their Work Better."**